Marsden Haddock and the Androides

Maynooth Studies in Local History

SERIES EDITOR Michael Potterton

You are reading one of the six volumes in the Maynooth Studies in Local History (MSLH) series for 2023. A benefit of being the editor of this series is the early opportunity to read a very wide variety of bite-sized histories covering events and activities from the magnificent to the outrageous in every nook and cranny of this remarkable island. This year's offerings take us from Bronze Age burials in west Kerry to a three-year dairy war in 1930s east Donegal, via an entrepreneur extraordinaire from late Georgian Cork, a revelatory survey of dire poverty in pre-Famine Westmeath, a century of exclusive terrace-life in colourful Tralee and the complex social networks of a family of Francophile Catholic landed gentry from Kildare. Together, these six studies take us on an astonishing journey on which we encounter smugglers, umbrella makers, lifelike automata, difficult marriage- and education choices, resolute defiance, agrarian violence, rapidly changing religious and political landscapes and a petition to have a region transferred from one nation to another.

These half-a-dozen volumes show how the 'local' focus of a *local history* can range from an individual person (Marsden Haddock) to a family (the Mansfields), a street (Day Place), a village (Portmagee), a county (Donegal and Westmeath) and beyond. The six authors have taken their stories from relative obscurity to centre stage. Denis Casey now joins Terence Dooley as one of only two people to have published three volumes in this series (though they are set to be joined by a third in 2024!).

This year in the Department of History at Maynooth University we are celebrating seventy years of excellence in teaching, research and publication (1953–2023) and we are especially delighted to be relaunching our enormously successful MA in Local History. Theses from this programme have traditionally provided the backbone of the MSLH series and we look forward to another rich crop in the years to come.

Whether you ask Alexa, ChatGPT or Raymond Gillespie, there is no doubting that Local History is valuable and significant. AI has evolved considerably since I grew up on a dairy farm in south Co. Meath and it is sure to play an increasing role in the research, writing and dissemination of local history. As with so many new technologies, of course, the greatest challenge is perhaps going to be maximizing the potential of Artificial Intelligence without compromising the integrity of the results.

Maynooth Studies in Local History: Number 163

Marsden Haddock and the *Androides*: entertainment, late Georgian Cork and the wider world

Neil Cronin

FOUR COURTS PRESS

Set in 11.5pt on 13.5pt Bembo by
Carrigboy Typesetting Services for
FOUR COURTS PRESS LTD
7 Malpas Street, Dublin 8, Ireland
www.fourcourtspress.ie
and in North America for
FOUR COURTS PRESS
c/o IPG, 814 N Franklin Street, Chicago, IL 60610

ISBN 978-1-80151-096–7

Printed in Ireland
by SprintPrint, Dublin

Contents

Acknowledgments

I wish to thank the staff of the Cork County Library, the Boole Library, University College Cork and the Royal Irish Academy for their assistance; the British Library for increasing access to their digital newspaper archives during the Covid-19 lock-down; and Sean Cronin for drawing maps of Haddock's itinerary. I also express my appreciation to Dr Michael Potterton as editor of the Maynooth Studies in Local History series for his guidance and patience and to the anonymous reviewers for suggestions about content.

Introduction

The late eighteenth and early nineteenth centuries were an era of unprecedented change – social, economic, cultural and political – with population growth, expanding urbanization, increasing wealth and disposable income and, for many people for the first time, designated free or leisure time. In fast-moving and uncertain times, there was less satisfaction with old standbys. Popular culture evolved accordingly. The appetite for novelty in a fickle audience was not easily sated – the journey from innovative to stale was short. The ability to anticipate, or to latch on to, trends was necessary to survive in a rapidly moving world.

Popular entertainment is a convenient label for commercially organized, performance-centred shows and spectacles of which there was a huge variety – music hall, circus, fairground amusements, exhibitions and numerous other events. While often overlapping with the 'legitimate theatre', contemporary observers recognized each as a separate entity. Such shows, usually entailing an admission charge, were becoming in Ireland as in Britain a growing part of popular culture. Its commercial impact was expanding, with growth in the amount and range of entertainment available and greater audience attendance from a widening social base. The audiences far-surpassed in number the more-studied reading and theatre-going public.[1]

Much popular entertainment took the form of exhibitions, where people paid to gaze at displays of pictures, objects or living creatures, including human beings. The spectrum at one end included scientific exhibitions and art collections to, at the other, freak shows of the weird and wonderful, with fascination with peculiarities of the human form, often grotesque anomalies of anatomy or physiology. For the uneducated, exhibitions were an alternative to books and newspapers – in many cases, providing access to material and information hitherto confined to the literate. For the literate, they represented a supplement to books, offering in physical form what was contemporary in popular culture or current affairs, for example pictorial narratives of the voyages of exploration or of recent momentous events in history.

Before the turn of the century, most touring entertainments in urban Ireland were theatrical. Exhibitions were occasional visitors to Cork, albeit usually only after more affluent population centres had been fully exploited. Sometimes, its geographical location gave the city unique opportunities. The *Golden Grove* was a transport ship in the First Fleet, a convoy of eleven ships that brought the first settlers and convicts to Australia. On its return in 1789 carrying the scientific spoils of the expedition, it disembarked in Cork. Although bound for the royal collection in London and not designed for public exhibition, the captain was prevailed upon to exhibit the contents to the good people of Cork. A show entitled the *Curiosities of Botany Bay* displayed stuffed birds and beasts such as parakeets, leopards and seahorses, drawings of aboriginal war weapons, as well as charts and maps of this new world. Among the exhibits were 'some live kangaroos of different sizes', likely the first seen in Europe. The exhibition was from ten o'clock each morning to three in the afternoon, with an admission charge of 2*s*. 8*d*. The ardour of the naval officers to enlighten the citizens of Cork may have been cooled by the mysterious disappearance of several exotic birds from the display. At the other end of the spectrum, the Double-Jointed Dwarf came to Cork, possessed of such strength that he had lifted and carried O'Brien, the Irish Giant.[2]

One type of exhibition entering its heyday was displays of mechanical ingenuity. The Industrial Revolution was cranking into top gear. Uncertain times brought forth great innovation and all seemed possible to the inventive mind. Often the most successful examples of creativity were expended on apparent trifles. The poorly educated and superstitious gazed at automatons and other life-like figures with wonder and often fear. For the more sophisticated, the challenge was to detect the mechanisms that gave such a convincing appearance of animation.

The hero of this story is Marsden Haddock of Cork, who devised a show of mechanical figures, the *Androides*. His career coincided with the height of the automaton craze at the end of the eighteenth and the first decades of the nineteenth century. Such exhibitions were occasional visitors to Ireland and the young Haddock was very likely inspired during his formative years by exposure to examples of the mechanical arts. Maybe as a youth he was taken to see James Cox's celebrated Museum of Automata on its visit to Dublin in 1774. The twelve pieces on display were exquisitely constructed, the beauty of the external appearance matching the intricacy of the internal mechanisms. Swans and boats glided serenely through water, against a background of the stars in the firmament, all in motion in time to music. Mechanical flautists played solos and duets, the movement of the mechanical fingers true to the melody. The pinnacle of the display was a pair of life-sized peacocks, whose feathers spectacularly fanned-out, described modestly by Cox as 'a miracle of Art'.[3]

Less frequently, such exhibitions came to Cork. In 1790, at Heffernan's Great Room near the Exchange, among the exhibits Mr Manuel displayed was the Italian Fantoccini, or puppet show, 'performed with curious figures, not exceeding 22 inches in height ... [with] surprising feats of posturing and tumbling'. More amazing still were the 'mechanical figures consisting of the original automaton, the Sympathetic Figure, the Italian Lady and the self-moving Chariot'.[4]

A few years later, one of the most renowned exhibitions visited Cork. The *Eidophusikon* was devised by the English actor David Garrick and created by French painter Philip James de Loutherbourg. A runaway success in London on its opening in 1781, its touring version reached Cork in 1792. A forerunner of cinema, displaying 'moving pictures', the *Eidophusikon* was set up as a large-scale miniature theatre. The special effects were achieved by mechanical means, with mirrors and pulleys, creating a near-perfect illusion of movement. Most popular were scenes of sunrise and sunset, moonlight, storms and volcanoes. The show in Cork contained a new vista, 'Plymouth Sound at noon-day'. The 28th regimental band of the Cork garrison provided the music and sound-effects for the show, remarkable for its realism, including the early morning bird chorus, all-in-all providing a 'grand presentation of the most interesting phenomena of nature'.[5]

Uniquely for the time, Haddock's entertainment originated in Ireland, from where he toured Britain and America, with for many years considerable success. The extent of his travels and touring on both sides of the Atlantic were near-unprecedented. He was an engaging character. In the face of recurrent setbacks, he was distinguished by ingenuity, versatility and resilience. This work seeks to position Haddock and the origin of his entertainment in the context of the time and place of late Georgian Cork, and to use the ready reception of his entertainment as an illustration of the integration of urban Cork into the wider English-speaking world of the time.

1. Marsden Haddock and Cork

Born about 1759, Marsden Haddock started work in the late 1770s, training under his father Edward at their workplace and shop at Fenn's Quay. As indicated by the sign of the chair outside the premises, Edward was a furniture-maker. Cork city and its commodious harbour were, in times of war, among the busiest transit centres of the Atlantic world, with constant traffic in British army and navy and merchant-shipping officers. As well as offering all that the housekeepers of Cork might require, Edward specialized in portable collapsible furniture of his own manufacture, suitable for army-camp or ship life, as well as other intricate pieces such as venetian blinds.[1]

It was as one of the first umbrella makers in Cork that his son Marsden made his mark. Umbrellas of the eighteenth century were contraptions of crude construction. The articulated skeleton was made of whalebone or of wooden rods, and the canopy of oiled-silk or wax-coated canvas. The whole apparatus was heavy and cumbersome to use, difficult to open when wet and liable to crack when dry. To make a serviceable model required ingenuity and skill.[2] In a city prone to deluge, umbrellas were not the only commercial opportunity in water-resistance: dealing as he did in oil-cloth and other impermeable materials, Marsden offered protective travelling wear, hammer cloths, large tents, hat covers and water-proof covers for musical instruments; his 'new silk bathing caps [were] the best ever made in this city'[3] – all created at his Umbrella and Oil-cloth Manufactory. Another skill he possessed that enhanced the quality of his umbrellas was that of wire-drawer, fashioning wire from metals such as iron, brass and copper.[4]

Marsden had another calling that raised him above the level of a mere artisan and shopkeeper – from the early 1780s he built, installed and maintained organs. The organ was at its height of popularity in the eighteenth century. It was considered an acceptable instrument for females, whereas playing string or wind instruments was frowned upon. Highly rated as an organ builder, Haddock made organs 'of any construction, or to fit any situation'. Self-playing barrel-organs were a favourite, 'fit for a small church, chapel or chamber', for 'pleasuring parties' or 'chiefly for dancing'. One of the more innovative, built for Ballymyrtle church in 1790, played psalms, anthems and volunteers. Costing thirty guineas, it was 'a convenience where performers are not at hand'. Haddock moreover supplied finger keys so that 'any person who [played] the harpsichord [could] accompany the service of the church'.[5]

For larger or pipe-organs, the market in Cork was limited and they were usually commissioned. Church of Ireland parishes were numerous but with small congregations. The organ he built for the church in Upper Shandon was 'highly approved of' and received with 'spirited encouragement ... and approbation'.[6] As his reputation became established, he worked in cathedral churches and travelled further afield.

Relative to the number of adherents, Catholic places of worship in Cork were few. The Augustinians in Brunswick Street (present-day St Augustine Street) were the first to have an organ in a Catholic chapel in Cork. The instrument had been mute for several years until resuscitated by Haddock. He was indirectly responsible for another Catholic chapel acquiring an organ. In 1804, he offered for raffle an organ of his own construction to 150 one-guinea ticket-holders. James Haly, bookseller and Catholic publisher at the Exchange, won the prize, which he duly passed on to the Franciscan chapel in Cross-street (Liberty Street).[7]

At the time, raffling was a popular combination of both promoting and selling one's wares. After James Cox had displayed his celebrated Museum of Automata to Dublin in 1774, he placed many of his creations into such a lottery.[8] In 1784, Haddock, 'at very great trouble, expense and loss of time', constructed a finger organ, according to his claim the first made in the in city, which he raffled between eighty one-guinea ticket-holders; another for a less elaborate instrument between twenty-six one-guinea subscribers. In 1795, he raffled a harpsichord made by the celebrated Rucker, with fifty tickets at two guineas each. He also offered second-hand barrel organs for sale and harpsichords for hire, and tuned and maintained all keyboard instruments.[9]

Haddock was himself an accomplished organist. His impromptu performance at the inauguration of the refurbished instrument in the

Augustinian chapel was greatly admired. He was formally appointed an organist in a city church and respectfully declined another offered at St Peter's.[10] Throughout his touring career, the organ and its music were always a central part of his shows.

In 1785, Edward transferred his business to Hanover Street, leaving his son the sole occupier in Fenn's Quay. In 1792, Marsden too moved to a new location, to nearby Castle Street, next to the Exchange, then the administrative and retail centre in Cork. Haddock had a weakness for poor-quality verse. Hudibrastic verses composed in honour of the new undertaking were an encyclopaedic listing of the products produced and sold in his new emporium. The novel retail feature was glass – 'His shop is now completely stored/With choicest glass from Waterford/Decanters, Rummers, Drams and Masons/Flutes, Hob Nobs, Crofts and Finger Basons', followed by an exhaustive inventory of rhyming glass products. The ever-resourceful Haddock cut the glass himself as well as employing a cutter from England. As with all Haddock's business ventures, the new shop aimed at the higher end of the market. Among other products in his vast catalogue were further musical instruments, from the guitar to the bagpipes, Dutch wooden clocks, fishing and shooting sporting-goods, writing materials and the best Dublin snuff. While the premises in Castle Street was a cornucopia of his merchandise, that 'those who to visit him incline/will find an organ for his sign' suggests the organ business to him remained paramount. Notwithstanding his several commercial interests, for the adventurous and versatile Haddock, a new career beckoned.[11]

Among the mechanical exhibitors, there was a fondness for neologisms of classical origin, providing a veneer of class. A few such as *panorama* have survived into modern usage – the Panorama of London and the Grand Panorama of the battle of the First of June were alternative attractions to Haddock's in Cork. The word *Androides* – literally, a form of man – chosen by Haddock to describe his figures was not of recent coinage, however, having been recorded first in Chambers dictionary in 1728, where it was defined as a 'figure of a man which by virtue of certain springs &c. duly contrived walks, speaks &c'. Haddock popularized the word and, for the years he was active, the designation *Androide* was synonymous with Haddock and his machines.[12]

Cork's social, cultural and legal life orbited around the twin suns of the assizes, the visits of the higher courts to the city twice a year. The summer assizes marked the opening of the theatre season, the annual climax of Cork's social year, when conviviality and distraction continued for several weeks. Balls and ridottos, an opportunity for courtship and match-making, were even more vibrant during the war years, embellished as they were with dashing soldiery. Country gentlemen had the opportunity to gather and debate the issues of the day. The settling of accounts and visits from customers of the optimum type gave the retail trade a twice-yearly boost. The heightened political activity of the early decades of the nineteenth century brought forth Catholic aggregate meetings at every assize, where Daniel O'Connell perfected his oratory. The official function of the assizes was to hear cases of the higher court of the city and county, and to transmit government policy through the magistrates. More often than not, the culmination of the assize season was that most gruesome of popular exhibitions, always assured of an attendance of multitudes, public executions on Gallows' Green.[13]

The grand opening of the new entertainment – *Haddock's Exhibition of Androides; or, Wonderful imitations of human nature* – added great novelty to the spring assizes of 1794. He set up in a large room in his own umbrella manufactory in Castle Street. There were five shows daily, at 12 and 2 o'clock during the day and 7, 8 and 9 o'clock in the evening, each lasting less than one hour. The admittance charge was 1s. 1d.[14]

Denis Driscol, a radical republican ideologue, was editor of the *Cork Gazette*. While they were strange bed-fellows, both could lay claim to be children of the Enlightenment. Driscol was a frequent and enthusiastic advocate for Haddock, his innovation and inventiveness a reflection of the Enlightenment values the radical editor espoused, the application of scientific principles for education and 'rational entertainment'. 'How great our admiration when we are told of astonishing curiosities to be seen in foreign countries. We lament our misfortune in being placed so far from such wonders ... [but] we have at home with us, at the Mechanic Theatre, Castle Street, works of such ingenuity as would do honour to the most polished nation at any period'.[15] Driscol's levelling philosophy may have been less to the liking of the capitalist Haddock.

After some weeks, Haddock visited Limerick to exhibit and possibly elsewhere, returning to Cork in September. His entertainment had evolved, with 'additions made to his mechanisms'. There were now three shows a day of one hour and a quarter duration, at 1, 3 and 8p.m. in Castle Street. As winter came, a grand fire was maintained in the room for the patrons. Another pattern was set in a stream of favourable press coverage – 'the first scientific judges of mechanical powers are not alone entertained but astonished'.[16] Crowds flocked daily. Haddock claimed to be due in Dublin in early winter and would exhibit in Cork for four weeks only. In late October, he announced he was delayed four weeks. In mid-December he announced the last week of the *Androides* in Cork. On Christmas Eve, Haddock added another week although this would delay his visit to Dublin. He showed into January and did not appear in Dublin until mid-March. These early and repeated declarations of impending closure became a standard tactic to encourage attendance.[17]

These early appearances were trial-runs, learning on the job and finessing his showmanship, before taking on more challenging commercial opportunities. The cosmopolitan audience of Dublin, the second city of the empire, with its vice-regal court, parliamentary houses of lords and commoners, gentry and monied classes, presented a lucrative opportunity for Haddock. Now styling himself the 'proprietor and inventor of the *Androides*', he opened in Dublin in March 1795 at the Lyceum on College Green. As was his wont, on arrival, he threatened impending departure: 'his stay in Dublin must be very short, as he carries on an extensive manufacturing business, which requires his personal attendance'.[18] During the run, he re-titled the venue the 'Mechanic Theatre', a designation he continued to use throughout his career. The exhibition had further evolved, reaching its mature format, with a longer duration of nearly two hours, with now two shows daily, afternoon and evening. The admittance charge had also increased, boxes 3s. 3d., pit 2s. 2d. and gallery 1s. 1d.[19]

Haddock spent three months in the capital from mid-March to mid-June 1795. Press coverage was again uniformly positive: he 'met with unparalleled success in this city'; 'never was an exhibition more admired in this city … a crowded fashionable audience twice every day … the most wonderfully ingenious and the best imitation of real life such principles ever yet produced'.[20]

While in Dublin, Murtogh O'Blarney composed 'a poetical description of his mechanism' for which Haddock gave sincere thanks. In its honour, Haddock reproduced the verses in a handbill, free for paying customers, but otherwise a one-penny charge. These provide the first description of Haddock's *Androides*. At this time, before he went to London, his pieces were the Spelling automaton, the Fruitery, Liquor Merchant and Highland Oracle.[21] It is apparent from O'Blarney's verses that his subsequent performances changed little if any from this Dublin show.

On returning from Dublin, Haddock again showed in Cork, the third occasion within 18 months, again at his Castle Street premises. He was uncharacteristically bullish – 'price of admission will be only 1s. 1d., even to children, nor will he lower his price during his stay'.[22] He opened on this occasion during the summer assizes, likely the reason he had hurried back, during which he had three shows a day. As the gentry and landed families departed for the country after the assizes, the crowds fell off, and he reverted to two shows a day, and later an evening show only. A stratagem he often deployed as attendance was falling was ominously to declare he had to 'finally close, perhaps for ever'. More often than not, something turned up to save the day: 'on account of some new machinery he is making for England is under the necessity of staying longer than he expected'. This Cork run finally finished in late October 1795.[23]

London, to where Haddock was about to travel, was a magnet for those with cultural ambitions. Exhibiting the *Androides* in the largest city in the world was a considerable career step. Always ambitious and adventurous, early success likely boosted confidence in his new product. The primary motivation was of course financial, an opportunity to make money, to service either future plans or past debts. However, leaving Cork entailed risk.

Cork thrived on war – even the rumour of war was good for business.[24] Near-continuous conflict between France and England from 1740 to 1815 was a bonanza for the economy of the city, its harbour and agricultural hinterland. The prosperity of the war-fuelled economy filtered down the socio-economic pyramid, but provided the richest nourishment to the upper levels. Economic growth caused an expansion in particular of the retailing and manufacturing trades, and of the service industries. The emergence of secondary professions such as lawyers, accountants, bankers, architects and dentists was particularly noticeable. The profusion of the newly monied intensified competition in the retail trade, each fighting for their share of expanding disposable income. The number and diversity of shops increased – Haddock's was not the only emporium the war-economy gave birth to. James Haly his neighbour in Castle Street, as booksellers tended to do, dabbled in numerous areas and in addition now opened a Music and Musical Instrument Warehouse, which included pianos and several other instruments. He was agent for William Southwell of both Dublin and London, one of the most innovative of piano-makers.[25]

There were other organ builders and sellers in Cork. Robert Murdock worked between Cork, Dublin and London, and tuned, built and sold organs, harpsichords and the increasingly fashionable piano-forte.[26] Henry Laycock built an even greater variety of musical instruments; he had trained in London, where he maintained connections while in Cork. Whether Haddock trained under, or worked with, or used the London connections of, these individuals is not known. Commercial rivalry and the rising popularity of the piano were encroaching on Haddock's primary commercial concern, the organ business.[27]

Commercial life, even in wartime Cork, was difficult. For his work on the church organ in Upper Shandon, it took Haddock at least two years to get paid. Obliged to resort to a public notice, he 'humbly begged the gentlemen who composed the committee for raising subscriptions for payment of said organ … to adapt some mode of paying him the remaining sum of £139 16s. 10d.'[28] Such parsimony for work done from even church authorities must have enhanced the sound of jangling coins at the box-office *before* the show. One can speculate as to his other motivations. Whether he then saw the *Androides* as a temporary dalliance or a long-term commitment is unclear. Whatever his intent, he stayed in London for longer than he had originally planned.

2. London and back to Cork

Before giving an account of what was his greatest commercial success, it is opportune to describe Haddock's mechanical pieces, the *Androides*, as they appeared in London, the entertainment capital of the world, and to examine their lineage.

Who created the *Androides*? The credit was usually bestowed on Haddock: 'The fertile brain of Mr Haddock, the ingenious proprietor, cannot cease from invention'. Haddock was undoubtedly happy to accept the accolades: from early in his career, he styled himself the 'proprietor and inventor of the *Androides*'. He claimed 'the Principles of Action are entirely new'. History has been less kind. According to Harry Houdini, a historian of magic as well as its most renowned exponent, 'Haddock had no particular standing in the world of magic, and it is more than likely that he rented the automata which he exhibited, or merely acted as showman for the real inventors'.[1]

There is a distinction to be made between true automaton figures, such as the Writing and Spelling Figures, and his other pieces, often termed mechanical assemblages. An automaton is a mechanism that performs a pre-determined range of functions according to an inserted set of coded instructions. Haddock had exhibited the Spelling Automaton from the beginning. The Writing Automaton was introduced as part of his entertainment in London, to no little acclaim: 'we may assert that Pope's Dunciad does not exhibit a wooden-headed genius so expert at his pen as the Writing Automaton'.[2] The automatons opened the show.

THE WRITING AUTOMATON – A figure about the size of a boy of five years old, will be brought to a table, and set to write any word, words or figures required, in a round legible hand.[3]

The eighteenth century saw a succession of renowned continental automaton inventors. The Frenchman Jacques de Vaucanson in

1742 displayed in London music-playing automatons, a flute player, drummer and piper. The most-renowned creator of automaton figures was the Swiss watchmaker Pierre Jaquet-Droz. With his three automaton figures of a writer, draughtsman and harpsichord player, he came to London in 1776. These creations were a wonder of the age. Replicas were made to optimize their commercial potential and toured Europe well into nineteenth century. His was the first and most famous writing figure.[4] Powered by clockwork mechanics, the automaton had 6,000 separate parts and contained forty replaceable interior cams. Cams are discs of varying size and shape that rotated on a cylindrical shaft. Follower-rods attached the cam discs to the moving part of the automaton, in this case the writing hand. Depending on the shape, size and rotation speed of each cam, and the length of the follower-rod, the writing hand reliably and repeatedly performed a specific movement. Depending on the cam design and selection, any letter or series of letters could be inscribed by the automaton. The mechanism possessed the additional capability that its eyes followed the goose-feather quill inscribing the letters. This represented a basic but effective form of programming that even today is unsettling in its realism.[5] It was a version of this piece that Haddock had in his London exhibition.

Henri Maillardet from about 1791 was the London representative of Jaquet-Droz, the proprietor for the British tours and also himself a creator of automatons. Maillardet ran his 'Magnificent Automatical Museum' in Spring Gardens from 1798 to 1817, open from 10 in the morning to 12 midnight, charging 2*s*. 6*d*. Another Jaquet-Droz automaton, the harpsichord player, was the most admired piece. Throngs of nobles and notables visited Maillardet's exhibition. His museum was even graced by a visit from the queen with her retinue of princesses and aristocratic retainers.[6] Haddock in London at the time never obtained such a mark of distinction and never had the prestige of a royal visit.

Maillardet was Haddock's rival, but may also have been his collaborator. Maillardet exhibited a writing automaton of the same description as Haddock's. As Houdini surmised, Haddock may have rented the piece from Maillardet. Haddock occasionally featured a drawing automaton or an automaton with both writing and drawing capability. 'A new movement has been put to the writing automaton whereby it also becomes a drawing automaton, and can be set to draw a clear outline of a lion, elephant, bear, camel, horse or stag'. Such was also an exhibit in Maillardet's Museum.[7] The suspicion is that Haddock was sufficiently skilled to operate and maintain, but not to create or construct, such a sophisticated automaton. He may have been reliant on technical support from his rival exhibitor. It is notable that after leaving London he never again displayed a writing or drawing automaton.

A cruder writing and drawing figure was constructed by the notorious Thomas Denton. After he was hanged for coining in 1789, this figure was sold by auction in London and, it has been suggested, purchased by Haddock.[8] That Haddock displayed the Writing Automaton only on coming to London makes Maillardet the more likely source.

THE SPELLING AUTOMATON – *a figure about three feet high, representing a female child, will be brought to a table, where an alphabet is placed, on which it will spell any given word.*[9]

The Spelling Figure was a more basic automaton. It too had to be programmed before responding to requests from the audience. 'The machine is wound up at the beginning, to put it in motion, and on the word or words being given, the machine is adjusted in a very short time by the exhibitor'.[10]

Although to point to a letter on an alphabet board did not require as sophisticated a mechanism as writing that letter, it was still a machine of some substance: 'the Spelling Automaton, though perhaps the most plain and simple of any, certainly commands a considerable share in the general excellence ... about three-foot high and can when wound up spell any word dictated to it in the English language. It is really curious to see this machine-girl cast her eyes down upon the alphabet, and spell any word with the greatest accuracy, and with a graceful demeanour'.[11] This automaton Haddock exhibited from the beginning to the end of his career. It is not known whether he acquired or constructed the spelling figure himself. There is no evidence of any other exhibitor displaying a similar figure.

Once the automatons had completed their entertainment, the assemblages were introduced. These induced in the audiences of the day more wonder than the true automatons.[12] Each had a long lineage, but, hampered by limited sources, self-promotion and newspaper puffery, it can be difficult to disentangle competing claims. Haddock's description of the first piece, the Fruitery, was as follows:

THE FRUITERY — *At the gate of which the* PORTER *stands, and when desired, rings the bell; then the* FRUITRESS *comes out to attend the company with any fruit demanded, at pleasure; it will likewise take in flowers, or any small articles, and produce them again as called for. The different fruits will be given in charge to a* WATCH DOG, *which barks on their being taken away, and ceases on their being returned. Next, the little* CHIMNEY SWEEPER, *comes from behind the house, enters the side door, presently ascends the chimney, and cries 'sweep!' several times, then descends and goes off with his bag full of soot.*[13]

In 1738 the Italian showman Balducci exhibited at the Red Lyon Tavern in Pall Mall a collection of novelties, with which he toured up and down the country for the following thirty years. Among them was a piece called the Druggist, 'which on command … opens the door and shows himself to the spectators; he gives to any spectator liberty to order him to bring any sort of drug he sells, viz., coffee, tea, sugar, cinnamon, cloves, nutmegs &c., and brings it to the spectator that ordered it'. Haddock's Fruitery was a variation and more elaborate version of Balducci's Druggist. Much admired, even the critical Houdini was impressed: 'Haddock's own description of the fruitery trick … was even more complicated than the famous Pastry Cook of the Palais Royal'. The additional features were likely Haddock's contributions.[14]

THE LIQUOR MERCHANT *and* WATER SERVER — *The* LIQUOR MERCHANT *stands at a cask, from which it will draw, at the choice of the company, any of the following liquors—rum, brandy, gin, whisky, port, mountain, shrub, raisin wine, peppermint, anniseed, carraway and usquebaugh. The* WATER SERVER *stands at a pump to supply water when ordered and pumps, or ceases, at the desire of any person present.*[15]

The Liquor Merchant also has a discernible ancestry. Henry Winstanley, famous for building the first Eddystone lighthouse, opened 'The Water Theatre' at Piccadilly about 1696. One of the attractions was the 'Wonderful Barrel', which 'will entertain the spectators with several sorts of liquids, hot and cold, suitable to the

season, and without mixture'. In 1713 it was announced that there
would be 'six sorts of wine and brandy coming out of the famous
barrel'. In 1710, in another iteration of the same trick, 'a "New
Mathematical Fountain", was described as being a tavern, a coffee-
house and a brandy-shop, which at command runs, at one cock,
hot and cold liquor, as sack, white wine, claret, coffee, tea, content,
plain, cherry and raspberry brandy, Geneva, usquebaugh and punch'.
In Haddock's version, the Liquor Merchant dispensed twelve spirits
from the one cask and spout. 'To show there is no deception, any one
is permitted to taste the liquors as they are drawn'.[16]

THE HIGHLAND ORACLE – *A figure in the highland dress, which gives a
rational answer, by motion, to any question proposed, calculates sums in
arithmetic, by striking its sword on a targe* [a light shield used by the Scots]*,
and gives the amount of any number of yards, pounds &c. at any given price;
strikes the hours and minutes, whenever asked, and also strikes the difference
of time between any watch and the time-piece on which it stands; beats time to
music &c.*[17]

Of all Haddock's pieces, the Highland Oracle was regarded as
'the most curious of all'. The Oracle occupied the last segment
of the show, suggesting it was the climax of the entertainment –
'This Caledonian Animated Automaton closes every exhibition
of the *Androides* ... with such delight and leaves such an indelible
impression on the minds of the audience that all the other ingenious
pieces (though equally interesting) are quite forgot'. As with all of
Haddock's figures, the Oracle was constructed with skill and artistry,
imbuing the figure with magisterial authority: 'the oracular power
of the Highland Chief is only equalled by the haughty toss of the
head, so characteristic of a Chief of a Clan'.[18] Again, this piece is
descended from Balducci's exhibits. The Italian had a piece named the
Blackmoor, which 'by striking with a hammer on a bell does all that
is commanded, and will guess the spectator's thought. The Highland
Oracle was the Blackmoor in another guise'.[19]

In summary, the Writing Automaton was designed and constructed
by the Droz-Maillardet organization and likely the Spelling Figure
was acquired rather than built by Haddock. Also, contrary to
claims of originality, Haddock's assemblages were evolutions or re-
arrangements of previous pieces, at least in part copies of what he

had either seen or read about, rather than his own creations. He was standing on the shoulders of his predecessors. The improvement on the mechanisms and appearances of previous models was substantial, however, and it would be harsh to deprive Haddock of credit for his contributions.

Who then built the assemblages? Given his artisan training and work experience, it was well within his compass to construct the pieces he exhibited. The exteriors of all his pieces were made of wood. Given his expertise in jointed umbrellas and parasols, movable folding furniture, intricate musical organs and wire-drawing, he certainly had the skill and ingenuity to construct the figures he exhibited. The sound effects of a figure crying 'sweep!' or of a barking dog, while regarded as remarkable and exciting genuine wonder at the time, were well within the capabilities of an experienced organ-maker. Similarly, a skilled wood-worker with experience and expertise in fine-bore tubes and water-resistant materials would not have found insurmountable the construction of such as the Liquor Merchant.

LONDON

Haddock opened his show at the Mechanic Theatre in Norfolk Street, off the Strand, in late 1795.[20] The Strand was then the centre of the entertainment world, full of theatres and coffee houses, tumultuous and always crowded. However, business during his first months in London was precarious. Haddock was usually skilled at charging what the market could bear, but occasionally misjudged. Admittance was ambitiously priced: boxes 4s. and gallery 2s. After several weeks, the admission charge was halved but business remained disappointing.[21] After a short three months in the great metropolis, Haddock declared his closing imminent as he 'must soon repair to his manufactory at home'. He was saved from a dispiriting early departure by a happy accident of geography. The annual Royal Academy Exhibition was held in Somerset House off the Strand from 1780 onward. The exhibition of 1796 opened on 23 April. William Turner, only one of the attractions that year, displayed ten watercolours and for the first time an oil-painting at the academy. Not alone were the crowds unprecedented but they brought to the vicinity of the Mechanic

Theatre customers of the optimum category: 'The number of Noblemen's carriages which fill Norfolk-Street every day ... during the time of exhibiting the *Androides* renders it the genteel lounge of the day', and 'the little theatre being nearly contiguous to Somerset House has greatly contributed to make it a place of fashionable resort and with propriety it may be asserted that the first circles have found themselves highly entertained'. The academy's exhibition gave Haddock an annual boost during the years he exhibited in London. His fortunes revived, Haddock resolved to continue 'until further notice'.[22]

After the uncertain start, the *Androides* garnered audience and editorial approval. In June 1796, Haddock again declared he was 'intent on leaving London' and the show would close in two weeks, so beginning another protracted farewell. Instead, he closed the morning show 'for the purpose of procuring time to execute some new pieces of mechanism, which he means to bring out next winter'. Later, business remaining strong, 'it would be imprudent in him to leave London as long as his Mechanic Theatre continues to be so crowded'. After several extensions to avoid 'disappoint[ing] so many respectable parties', he closed in late August so as to 'proceed on his projected plan for future operations ... [and] requests all accompts will be sent in for payment this week'. His projected plan for future operations was touring (fig. 1; table 1).[23]

Haddock's first stop was Bristol, then the second-most populous city in Britain. While in London, Haddock had continued his home operation and advertising in the Cork newspapers.[24] There being frequent sea traffic between Cork and Bristol, he may have spent some time in his hometown before his first incursion into provincial England.

In September 1796, he opened in Bristol, at Taylor's Hall in Broad Street, soon re-christened the Mechanic Theatre, with the same format including both the writing and spelling figures. He next visited Bath – with its wealthy clientele the likely purpose of his excursion out of London – where he showed for four months. There Haddock was favoured with a visit by the duke and duchess of York and, as a sign of their approval, allowed use of their arms in his promotions. Such a mark of royal patronage greatly impressed the Cork newspapers, not least the republican Driscol. Haddock next exhibited for some weeks

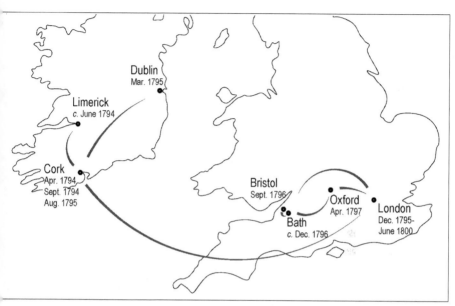

1. Haddock's touring itinerary, 1794–1800

Table 1. Haddock's touring itinerary, 1794–1800

1794	Apr.	Cork
	?	Limerick
1794–5	Sept.–Jan.	Cork
1795	Mar.–June	Dublin
	Aug.–Oct.	Cork
1795–6	Dec.–Aug.	London
1796–7	Sept.–May	Bristol
		Bath
		Oxford
1797–8	June–Aug.	London
1798	Aug.–Sept.	Cork (not exhibiting)
1798	Sept.–June 1800	London
1800	June	Return to Cork

in Oxford, closing there in May 1797, before returning to London 'as he has his manufactory to attend to'.[25]

After a nine-months absence, Haddock returned to London in June 1797. He opened immediately on arrival, at first in a temporary venue, again on the Strand, maybe to catch the late Royal Academy crowds. The only change to his show was a 'new Spelling automaton

[that] gives great satisfaction'. By August, he was back at his usual location at 38 Norfolk Street.[26]

Haddock announced his intention of 'fixing his residence in this great metropolis ... determined to exert himself as an organ builder and machinist to the utmost of his abilities to bring forward inventions, both useful and entertaining'. He offered 'table organs of different kinds and prices made and invented by Haddock'. This transfer of Haddock's organ construction was at least several months in planning, as the move had been announced in the Cork newspapers the previous January: Haddock 'has opened an organ manufactory in London where he has an opportunity of executing the instruments to his own wish'. There was no intention of abandoning his Cork business – the shop in Castle Street continued to take orders 3½ to 400 guineas and upwards.[27]

The London audience was not sated and the *Androides* rapidly regained their previous popularity. It was necessary to reserve places several days before. The theatre was too small for the numerous visitors and often people were turned away at the evening show. By winter, it was reckoned Haddock would need three performances each day 'when the town fills'.[28]

Almost all of Haddock's exhibiting career in Britain was during the cataclysmic events and existential crises of the French Revolutionary and Napoleonic wars. The French wars tested the resolve of the British nation but their response was one largely of patriotic fervour and of solidification of the sense of British nationalism. Not the least of the consequences of burgeoning patriotism was the commercial opportunities afforded the entertainment industry. Even the inanimate *Androides* were not immune to the pervasive patriotic exhilaration. The Writing Automaton had 'a touch of the heroics [and] can scarce write any words but the name of Admiral Duncan or Admiral Jervis', the victorious commanders at the battles of Camperdown and Cape St Vincent respectively. The Liquor Merchant took to dispensing grog rather than spirits to the assembled company.[29]

Like the *Androides*, Haddock was not found wanting. He invented a new mechanism, the Telegraph, which became among his most popular. The piece was anachronistically named, as it was a semaphore system rather than electric telegraphy still some decades in the offing. At the beginning of the French wars, communication between the

Admiralty in London and the dockyard in Portsmouth took at best five hours, at the cost of the horses' exhaustion. Conscious that France had a communication system that spanned the country, in 1795 the Admiralty accepted a semaphore system. The semaphore frame was mounted on hastily erected buildings, usually on prominent hills. Thirteen intermediate stations linked London and Portsmouth. The wooden frame contained six 'windows' with moveable shutters. The shutters in either open or closed positions gave sixty-four options (two to the power of six), comprising the letters of the alphabet, the numerals o to 9, and the reminder commonly used naval terms. Signals could be transmitted at speed: a message from London to Portsmouth took no more than fifteen minutes. The system was used until the end of the Napoleonic wars.[30]

The first station of the London–Portsmouth line was visible to all Londoners, a wooden cabin atop the Admiralty in Whitehall, not far from the Mechanic Theatre. Haddock made its replica a part of his exhibition.

> This piece of mechanism represents the model of that on the Admiralty, with the cabin underneath where the officer sits to work it, which by the combination of six swivel boards can spell any word or enumerate any number of figures, exclusive of several occasional signals adapted for the purpose. The hand-bills give a description of the number of signals, and how they are combined to make a sentence.[31]

The effect of the Telegraph in London was near-sensational: the 'new piece, the Telegraph, has raised the curiosity of the polite and scientific world in a most astonishing manner',[32] and remained so throughout his subsequent touring. He sometimes had a version of the French telegraph in the show and the two systems communicating was a source of yet greater perplexity: 'every signal used by the Admiralty is deciphered with astonishing precision, and one telegraph made to answer the other with the utmost accuracy'.[33] Given the state of our present-day technological advancement, it can be difficult to apprehend the novelty and excitement of non-verbal communication. To our knowing eyes, such a device seems mundane but at the time was revolutionary. Haddock may have taken particular pride in the

Telegraph – most of his pieces had a long ancestry, but the Telegraph was the one most likely to have been entirely his own work.

The Battle of Camperdown between the British North Sea Fleet under Admiral Adam Duncan and the Dutch fleet was fought in October 1797. Signalling made a significant contribution to the overwhelming British victory. In July the following year, in Haddock's greatest promotional success, Lord Duncan himself attended the *Androides*. In the conquering hero's honour, the Telegraph signalled to engage the Dutch fleet. 'The hearts of all persons present seemed elate with joy on recollecting the memorable event'. While not as valuable in promotional currency as a visit from the royal family, a naval hero in the audience was a very worthwhile inducement: Haddock's show 'experiences every day and every night an overflow … ever since that theatre of ingenuity has been honoured with the presence of Lord Duncan and his family'.[34]

In the spring of 1798, Haddock announced his intention to depart London, addressed as usual to the nobility and gentry: 'business at home obliges him to be punctual in closing the *Androides*'. His departure was again protracted, whether because attendance had received a boost from Duncan's visit or because events in unsettled Ireland had dissuaded him from travelling. On this occasion, his resolve to quit London was determined: he sold off his remaining organs – 'a few table organs and a portable coach-organ will be sold cheap'; he requested the settling of outstanding accounts; and advertised the premises in Norfolk Street to be let, furnished or unfurnished, or the interest to be sold. In early August, after several missed deadlines, Haddock shut the Mechanic Theatre in Norfolk Street and returned to Cork, seemingly for good.[35]

The success of the *Androides* in the metropolis had not deflected him from his core business. Variously styling his business in Castle Street as Haddock's *Umbrella and Bathing Cap Manufactory* or as his *Umbrella, Oil Cloth and Organ Manufactory*, he had continued to manufacture, trade and advertise in Cork: 'best twilled silk and linen bathing caps, bathing and sporting tents, garden stools, and parasols on walking canes for the summer'; 'coach Parasols as made use of in Bath, London and Dublin'; and 'water-proof bathing caps, his much-improved umbrellas, his patent joint parasols, and his various shaped travelling dresses'. Having been in London, he had the advantage of access to 'better goods at no advanced price'. He highlighted the high-quality silk available to him in the metropolis. To embellish the accoutrement of the recently mustered Cork yeomanry, he offered helmet hoods, dragoon cloaks and military packs.[36]

Haddock's decision to return to Cork in 1798 seemed final. He declared to his fellow citizens that in London he had 'used every exertion to improve himself as an organ-builder and mechanic'. He asked the people of Cork to honour him 'with the care, repairs or improvement of any of the church organs' and gave assurances 'that his efforts to please [would] be found fully adequate'.[37] However, he rapidly abandoned his plans to re-settle in his native place. His youngest son, also Marsden, was born about 1797. Family commitments may account for his apparent indecision and erratic movements in these years. A more likely scenario is that the atmosphere of a much-disturbed Cork was neither what he had expected nor to his liking.

According to another traveller in that summer of 1798

> we proceeded to Cork, a little after the battle of Vinegar Hill. I saw many heads of the rebels stuck on the spikes over the gates of the city. Their long hair was let loose, and waved in the wind, which formed a very striking and terrific appearance.[38]

Soon after his arrival, four militia men were executed on the Mardyke in front of the entire garrison and a vast concourse of the populace. At the assizes that summer, there were numerous executions and transportations. At the end of August, Humbert and a French army landed in Killala, followed within a few days by a British defeat at Castlebar and the declaration of the provisional Republic of Connaught.[39] Although the Battle of Big Cross near Clonakilty, some weeks before Haddock's return, was the largest action of the rebellion seen in Cork, there remained widespread apprehension in the city that worse was to come.

Whatever the reason, after less than two months absence, he scurried back to London and soon re-entered the world of exhibition. The cover story for his absence was that he had

> for some weeks past been assiduously employed in improving and beautifying the different pieces of mechanism and the little

theatre, and they are now in such a state as he flatters himself will merit the favourable reception they have hitherto experienced from the curious.

He re-opened on 24 September 1798.[40] He continued to draw on the prevalent jingoistic fervour, adding further patriotic pieces to the cast of his show, now with new artistic elements. Haddock's short visit to Cork may explain these heightened creative endeavours – he had brought company back with him. While he was a pupil of the Cork-born James Barry at the nearby Royal Academy, the young John Corbet, a promising artist, lived with Haddock at Norfolk Street.[41]

In the eighteenth century, bonfires, fireworks and illumination were popular demonstrations of public celebration. In an age when any night without a moon was densely black, such occasions were a dazzling sight. As public lighting became more common, their effects were not as vivid and startling. To compensate, by the later years of the eighteenth century, transparencies had become a popular accompaniment to celebratory illuminations. Transparencies were scenes painted on a translucent substance, typically paper or lightweight cloth, such as silk, linen, calico or muslin. By means of bright lights placed behind them, they had a vivid and spectral effect. Haddock incorporated transparencies into the *Androide* show, Corbet contributing the artistry.

War kept providing inspiration and the Battle of the Nile spurred on the exhibitors further. In a piece incorporating transparencies, more akin to the *Eidophusikon* than a typical mechanical piece, the *Harlequin Magician* was a

> beautiful and interesting addition, which has lately enriched the representation of the Battle of the Nile ... The dismantling and sinking of the *Sérieuse* frigate, the firing from the fortifications, the appearance of the bombs, and the effect of their bursting are such unprecedented strides of optical and mechanical ingenuity as will doubtless continue to secure to this fashionable exhibition the same full attendance of splendour and nobility.[42]

The '*Harlequin Magician*, who displays several curious transparencies, is so great a favourite that several persons of the first distinction have thought it well worth a second and some even a third visit'.[43] Further patriotic transparencies were later added: 'some beautiful scenic representations … the taking of Seringapatam and the death of Tippoo, Britannia lamenting the death of Lord Howe, and Rolla restoring Cora her child (taken from the play of Pizarro)'.[44] The addition of Corbet's novel artistic elements gave the *Androides* fresh impetus: 'The action of automaton figures was hitherto the subject of much admiration, but the inventive genius of the *Androides* has set competition at defiance'.[45] Further artistic transparencies were produced. Among the triumphant illuminations in London after the surrender of the Batavian Navy, especially praised was that outside the Mechanic Theatre, 'a very brilliant transparency of the British fleet in the Texel, with the Dutch fleet in the background'.[46]

War also inspired further mechanical pieces. One was the Volunteer (fig. 2),

an automaton figure dressed in a military uniform, which appears at the gate of an antique building, called the Temple of Mars, and goes through the Manual and Platoon Exercise, by beat of drum (which is performed by an automaton drummer stationed for the purpose). It will then come out in any of the positions required, and concludes by firing off its musquet.

The bellicose bearing of the new piece drew great favour: 'The Volunteer seems to possess the fire of Mars himself, and by the explosion from his musquet, leaves the company enrapt in wonder and astonishment'.[47]

In September 1799, Haddock threatened closure again – he had 'some idea of removing the exhibition out of England'. There followed another protracted farewell. Repeated intimations of imminent closure may have suffered from diminishing returns. He finally resolved to close on 4 June 1800, the king's birthday, accompanied by more portentous foreboding: the *Androides* 'will be removed, probably for ever, from London'.[48] On this occasion, for once, the grim prediction proved correct. Strangely, despite only a few days remaining, he introduced a new piece, the Walking Minstrel, 'as large as life': 'A female figure five feet high that parades the stage in a graceful manner, accompanying any musical instrument with a

A NEW PIECE,

IS NOW EXHIBITED EVERY EVENING AT THE

ANDROIDES;

Or, Animated Mechanifm:

No. 38, NORFOLK-STREET, STRAND,

CALLED,

THE VOLUNTEER,

Being an AUTOMATON FIGURE dreffed in a Military Uniform, which appears at the Gate of an Antique Building, called

THE TEMPLE OF MARS,

And goes through the MANUAL and PLATOON EXER-
CISE, by beat of Drum, (which is performed by an AUTO-
MATON DRUMMER ftationed for the purpofe.) It will
then come out in any of the Pofitions required, and concludes
by firing off its Mufquet.

*Doors open every Day at Half paft Twelve, and the Performance begins at One;
and in the Evening opens at Half paft Seven, and begins at Eight.*

BOXES, 2s.——GALLERY, 1s.

The Pieces will be introduced in the following Order:—Firft,
The WRITING and DRAWING AUTOMATON;
Which can be fet to write any Word, or draw a clear Outline of any of the
following Beafts:—*A Lion, an Elephant, a Bear, a Tiger, a Horse, a Camel,
or a Stag.*
Second, THE VOLUNTEER, as above defcribed. Third,
THE TELEGRAPH,
A Defcription and Dictionary of which is given in the Bills prefented at the Theatre. Any
Perfon wifhing to become acquainted with the nature of that very ufeful Invention, the TELE-
GRAPH, will perfectly underftand it by once feeing this Exhibition. Fourth,
THE FRUITERY,
At the Gate of which the PORTER ftands, and when defired, rings the Bell; the FRUIT
RESS comes out to attend the Company with any of 12 different kinds of Fruit; it will like-
wife take in Flowers, or any fmall Articles, and produce them again as called for. Fifth,
The LIQUOR MERCHANT and WATER SERVER.
The LIQUOR-MERCHANT ftands at a Cask, from which it will draw, at the choice of the
Company, any of the following Liquors, *Rum, Brandy, Gin, Whifky, Port, Mountain, Shrub,
Raifin Wine, Peppermint, Annifeed, Carraway,* and *Ufquebaugh.* Sixth,
THE HIGHLAND ORACLE;
A Figure in the Highland Drefs, which gives a rational Anfwer, by Motion, to any Queftion
propofed, calculates Sums in Arithmetic, &c. &c.
The RUNNING ATTENDANTS (much improved) are Two Figures which wait on the
Company in the Gallery with any thing required from the Exhibition.
+++ Tickets to be had, and Places for the Boxes taken, at the MECHANIC THEATRE,
Norfolk-ftreet, which is neatly fitted up, lighted with Wax, and every Thing calculated to pleafe
a polite and difcerning Audience.
*** The Public are moft refpectfully informed, that from the intricacy of the Mechanifm
and Machinery of the New Piece, and the time required to prepare it, it can only be exhibited in
the Evenings; for the Day Exhibition the SPELLING FIGURE will be fubftituted in its ftead.

2. Haddock handbill from London (*c.*1799) promoting 'The Volunteer', a new addition
to his ensemble (Sotheby auctioneers)

triangle &c. &c.'[49] With the exception of touring in Bristol, Bath and Oxford, Haddock had exhibited in London almost continuously for four years.

As Haddock's *Androides* had an ancestry in London, so too had they an after-life. After elite shows passed their peak popularity, their productions frequently re-appeared in modified form for a more general audience, often in variety shows. At the end of his London escapade, Haddock sold the assemblages to Pietro Bologna, known as the Harlequin, who, with his sons, continued to exhibit them. In 1802, a variety show at the Private Theatre in Berwick Street, Soho, containing such as the 'Philosophical Fireworks, Phantasmagoria &c.', also included the Writing Automaton, Fruitery, Liquor Merchant, Caledonian Oracle and Walking Minstrel. In 1805, 'The *Androides* exhibited some years ago with great applause have been also ... added to the other amusements' of the *Pantascopia* at the Lyceum on the Strand, including the Telegraph, Liquor Merchant and Water-Server, which 'the proprietors of the above theatre have purchased at a great expense'. As late as 1820, Haddock's programme, including the Fruitery, continued to appear with only a few minor changes in the repertoire of Bologna at the Great Assembly Room, Three Tuns Tavern. The Fruitery had evolved further and is described thus: 'A curious Mechanical Fruiterer and Confectioner's Shop, kept by Kitty Comfit, who will produce at Command such Variety of Fruit and Sweetmeats as may be asked for'.[50]

There is no reason to believe Haddock intended anything other than returning to his previous life and had come home to Cork with the intention of staying. That he had unburdened himself of the *Androides* suggests he then had not the intention of exhibiting them again. He soon returned to his previous activities. In 1800, Haddock repaired the organ at St Anne's, Shandon, for £30, and another in Christ Church, South Main Street, in 1802, charging £63 11s. 3d. for refurbishment and maintenance. His shop in Castle Street stayed open until at least 1805 and raffles of musical organs continued as a promotional device.[51]

Cork remained on the exhibition touring circuit. One that would have piqued Haddock's professional interest was the visit from London of Mr Fairbrother's *Theatre of Astronomy* in 1803.

Astronomical lectures illustrated by the new *Dioastrodoxon*, or
grand transparent orrery ... assisted by mechanic elucidation of
the motion of the heavenly bodies ... rendering Astronomical
Truths so perspicuous that even those who have not so much
as thought upon the subject may acquire clear ideas of the
economy and harmony of the Planetary System.

This was perfect Enlightenment entertainment: 'The vicissitudes
of the seasons, and several other natural phenomena, difficult to
understand by verbal description alone, were explained with great
accuracy and simplicity by means of the machinery ... an instructive
and truly brilliant spectacle'. That Fairbrother thought his spectacle
'worthy of the attention and patronage of an enlightened, liberal and
discriminating public' was reflected in the prices – boxes 4*s*. 4*d*., pits
3*s*. 3*d*. and gallery 2*s*. 2*d*. The show was not a financial success: some
weeks later Haddock was selling tickets at his Castle Street premises
for the *Castle Spectre*, and a variety of other entertainments 'for the
benefit of Mr Fairbrother, who lately had the honour of delivering
his astronomical lectures to the ladies and gentlemen of Cork'.[52]

Haddock had a wide array of interests, all having in common
inventiveness and the lure of financial gain. Flourishing and
technology-based as it was, that 'the manufacture of paper has arrested
his particular concern' would not have been a surprise.[53] The paper
industry in Cork grew vigorously in the 1790s and the first decades
of the nineteenth century. Most prominent were the Sullivans, father
and son. The older rose from being a foreman in the Bagnell paper
mills to owning a thriving industrial enterprise of his own: at the
turn of the century, Sullivan was the largest paper manufacturer in
Ireland. Between all their enterprises, 2,000 people were employed.
Much of their produce was exported to England – he even won
a Treasury contract for printing Bank of England notes. Close to
Haddock's shop in Castle Street were many book, stationery and
paper shops. In a provocative move, Sullivan himself opened there a
retail outlet, selling paper and books. The new shop antagonizing his
wholesale customers, he was obliged to close.[54]

Haddock was ever innovative and resourceful. He invented a
largely automated process for the manufacture of paper, for which
he constructed experimental machinery. 'Mr Haddock of this city,

whose ingenuity as an artist is so generally known, has lately invented a mechanism for making paper, on such a plan as will enable the artificer to manufacture that article of better quality in less than one third of the time, and with fewer than one third of the hands usually employed in the ordinary method'. Presumably with the proceeds of the profits from his London residency, Haddock invested in a paper mill in Trantstown, on the Dublin Road between Glanmire and Watergrasshill. He improved the premises, re-building the interior, as well as erecting a dwelling-house, a drying-house and labourer accommodation, investing in all £1,300 in improvements. He was disappointed in the expectation of securing a patent for his new automated technology. For reasons unclear, Haddock became less involved. He rented out the premises for an annual £40. 'Afterwards induced to quit the country, he finally sold his interest for £100'. Details of the venture and its timeline are unclear but he likely lost substantial amounts of money.[55]

Haddock was not easily discouraged and retained his interest in paper manufacture. In 1811, he demonstrated paper products of novel manufacture to the Royal Dublin Society (RDS): 'specimens of paper made by him from vegetables, viz., paste-board made of English hay, paste-board made of Irish hay, approved of by the book-binders of Cork and paper manufacturers of Dublin; paper made of potato-stalks; ditto, of new hay; ditto, almost water-proof, of hay; ditto, of straw' and machines of his own construction for manufacturing paper and paper moulds from vegetable material.[56]

The French wars seemed never-ending. Stringent measures were introduced to finance the contest with Napoleon, including for the first time a tax on income. The economic nadir in wartime British economy was from the last months of 1810 to the autumn of 1812. Bankruptcies nationwide doubled.[57] The sister-island was even less robust in withstanding financial shock. The Cork newspapers of those years were peppered with notices of bankruptcies. Retail enterprises such as Haddock's were susceptible to any reduction in disposable income. The organ business too struggled, having the added disadvantage of the mounting dominance of the piano for home entertainment. Several new retail outlets for home-produced and imported pianos opened in Cork.[58] Listed as an organ builder and umbrella maker in Castle Street in 1805, by 1810 he had lost his shop and his niche in the Cork retail business.[59] His umbrella and related manufactory closed. That market was taken over by Solomon Hymes, who had an umbrella, sun-shade and oil-cloth manufactory in Broad Street, from where he replicated Haddock's output, down to even his line in silk and linen bathing caps. Haddock did however retain an interest in the organ business.[60]

Bad news accumulated. His daughter Jane Haddock, a milliner in Patrick's Street, was declared bankrupt in 1811. The Sullivan paper empire ran into difficulties in the later years of the war. To protect their workforce, they stayed afloat for a time with support from Dublin Castle but the business ultimately sank. James Haly, his neighbour at the Exchange, lost his newspaper, publishing and retail business. Even Solomon Hymes, Haddock's successor, floundered and he too was declared a bankrupt.[61]

ON THE ROAD AGAIN

Economically depressed Cork was no place for the entrepreneurial, but Haddock was maybe better off than others. He had in reserve tried-and-tested fallbacks to which he now resorted. The organ-installation business had remained healthy, money flowing from several years of top prices for the produce of the rich grasslands of south Munster and generous government subsidies given to the established church following the Act of Union, the First Fruits.[62] He installed new organs in the cathedral churches of both Ross and Cloyne. That in Cloyne had been imported and was erected by Haddock. The instrument had been 'particularly scaled for that church by Mr Haddock. It cannot be exceeded in point of tone, execution of style, or elegant taste and workmanship'. The replaced Cloyne organ was purchased by the parishioners of Youghal, who engaged Haddock to refurbish the instrument and erect it in their church, which, 'after passing through his hands, will appear quite another description of instrument'. Also, in 1810, he erected a new organ in Fermoy church.[63]

When organ installation allowed and ten years after he had seemingly retired, Haddock resumed exhibiting his 'animated mechanisms', the *Androides*. The likelihood is that he constructed a new set of assemblages. He may have retained the Spelling

Automaton as, unlike the other exhibits, there is no record of it being shown in London after his departure. In early May 1810, the *Androides* re-opened in Cork. As he no longer had his own premises in Castle Street, the Mechanic Theatre was now located near the Mail-Coach Hotel in Patrick Street. The admission charge was similar to previous: boxes 2*s*. 6*d*. and gallery 1*s*. 8*d*. Children were charged the same as adults. Despite claims of brisk business and of patrons turned away, the run of six weeks was short and only late were added two early shows each week. Tickets were to be had at his daughter's premises in Patrick Street. He had a new promotional feature – 'books giving a poetical and entertaining description of the exhibition with Telegraphic Dictionary', priced at one penny and published by William West, once his neighbour in Castle Street.[64] Not forgetting his organ business, he offered for sale a Gothic front-barrel organ with six stops, with patent drum and triangle, and three barrels of ten tunes each, principally modern country dances. Under pressure to construct the organ at Fermoy church, the *Androides* closed in June. For his final appearance in his native city, it was acknowledged that he 'has honoured the place of his nativity by his extraordinary acquirements in mechanics'.[65]

In the autumn of 1810, he was in Limerick. His admittance charge there was greater than usual, 3*s*. 4*d*. and 2*s*. 6*d*. 'Tickets and places to be had of Miss Haddock at the Clare Hotel, Bridge Street, where she will dispose of a variety of London haberdashery and millinery at very low prices'. 'Books describing the exhibition one penny' were available as they had been in Cork, and continued to be a feature of his entertainment until he went to America.[66]

Haddock opened in Dublin in February 1811, at the Mechanic Theatre in the Shakespeare Gallery off Grafton Street. Boxes were priced at 2*s*. 6*d*. and pits 1*s*. 8*d*. Business was brisk, with two shows each day. It was advised servants be sent to protect their masters' seats for them. There was continued demand for his table-organ.[67] After three months, business was falling off and in May closure was imminent. With his great powers of prescience, the Highland Oracle had predicted a visit from the vice-regal couple, the duke and duchess of Richmond. As the show was about to close, the lord lieutenant and his wife duly attended. 'Their graces testified unmixed satisfaction and yielded voluntary that their names may enrich the patronage by which Mr Haddock has been distinguished … we never witnessed an assemblage of more beauty, rank and fashion than filled the boxes and pit'. The names of the duke and duchess topped his advertisements. They presented tickets to their friends and even a second visit was contemplated. The visit led to a short-lived resurgence in attendance and the show closed in early July.[68]

After a gap of some months, again explained by organ installation, Haddock's Mechanic Theatre opened in Belfast before Christmas 1811, located at the Exchange coffee rooms. He expressed hopes that 'his being a Mechanic of the Irish soil will augment his claims on public patronage'. He enjoyed initial success and patrons were turned away, 'the theatre being but small'. 'The Marquis and Marchioness of Donegall … bestowed the most flattering encomium upon him'. Despite drawing good business, he left Belfast abruptly: he had 'received a letter from Cork' requiring him to return to complete an organ installation. Haddock began to wind down, closing in late February. Before his departure, he donated the proceeds of two shows to the Belfast Poor-House.[69]

While appearing in Belfast, the Cork newspapers expressed pride in his success: 'the genius of Mr Haddock will gather for himself and family some additional laurels from the field of mechanics'; and aware of his financial strictures were happy for him business was brisk: 'he has the consolation of reaping large remuneration from a grateful public'.[70]

3. Touring in Britain and America

His organ commissions complete, Haddock, now in his early 50s, was to spend the remainder of his life touring with the *Androides* (fig. 3; table 2). He no longer exhibited the Writing Automaton. With the exception of the addition of the Telegraph, he had essentially the same show as when he first exhibited in 1794, and this remained constant for the remainder of his exhibiting career. There were no more innovations. The greater part of the next six years was spent touring through Britain, at first in the larger cities and later in provincial towns. He never again exhibited in London, whether because the market was exhausted, the keenness of the competition, or by agreement with the competitors to whom he had previously sold his pieces.

In December 1812, the Mechanic Theatre opened in Fortune's Great Room in Prince's Street, Edinburgh. He had a successful three-month residency, with 'vast numbers disappointed'. Haddock next exhibited in Glasgow and Newcastle, and possibly in other towns. His arrival in York in August 1813 coincided with race week, and in late September he timed his arrival in Hull with the week of their annual fair. In December 1813, he was in Leeds – 'as the theatre is small, it is absolutely necessary that servants are sent timely to keep places'. There was unusually heavy snow that winter, but 'good fires are kept in the boxes'. It has been suggested that Luddite activity may have influenced his touring itinerary in Yorkshire and elsewhere.[1]

After a few months in Manchester, Haddock opened in Liverpool in June 1814, where the theatre was 'uncommonly crowded even to overflow'. After three months, he announced with his usual portentous declarations that he 'will shortly close for ever in Liverpool', as 'business in Cork requires his speedy return'.[2] As to what that business might have been, we have no information.

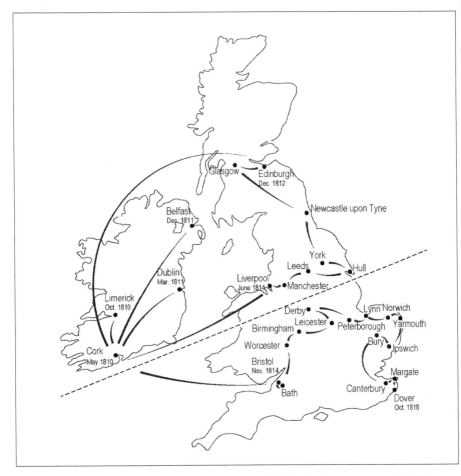

3. Tentative itinerary for the *Androides*, 1810–18. The dividing line separates Haddock's touring before and after his short return to Cork in 1814

After a few weeks in Cork, Haddock resumed his peregrinations in November 1815. After Bristol, he went to Bath; as in all those places he re-visited, on the second occasion, the show had a shorter run. We lose track of his movements for a year – Haddock was possibly touring in the south-west. He was in Worcester in early 1816, followed by stints in the midlands' larger towns.[3] In the summer of 1817, Haddock headed east, spending nearly a year travelling through East Anglia. While in Ipswich, his entertainment was suspended due to the death of Princess Charlotte. At the local obsequies, the muffled peal of the church bells was performed under Haddock's direction. In provincial

England, he continued with his usual format – two shows daily, the duration less than two hours, with 'no tedious interval to spread out the entertainment'. Admittance was boxes 2s. and gallery 1s., children under 12 at half-price. Also, when he could, he undertook organ work: 'Mr Haddock being an organ-builder would wish to devote his leisure time to repair and tune church, chamber, finger and barrel organs, or attend to tune piano-fortes'.[4] Haddock and the *Androides* by-passed London. He spent the summer season of 1818 at Margate. In the autumn of that year, he declared his intention of opening in Dover, which appears to have been his last show in England.[5]

Table 2. Tentative listing of Haddock's touring itinerary, 1810–18

1810	May–June	Cork
	c.Nov.	Limerick
1811	Mar.–July	Dublin
1811–12	Dec.–Feb.	Belfast
1812–13	Dec.–Mar.	Edinburgh
1813		Glasgow
		Newcastle
		York
	Sept.–Nov.	Hull
1813–14	Dec.–Feb.	Leeds
1814		Manchester
	June–Aug.	Liverpool
	Aug.–Oct.	Cork (not exhibiting)
	Nov.	Bristol
1815	Jan.–Feb.	Bath
	(whereabouts unclear)	
1816	Feb.	Worcester
		Birmingham
	Sept.–Oct.	Leicester
	Nov.–Dec.	Derby
1817		Peterborough
		Lynn
	May–June	Norwich
	Sept.	Yarmouth
	Oct.–Nov.	Ipswich
1817–18	Dec.–Jan.	Bury
1818	May	Canterbury
	Summer season	Margate
		Dover

AMERICA

Great claims have been made for Ireland in the Atlantic world: 'with
the possible exception of the Caribbean archipelago, no place was
less insular and more directly affected by the complex circulation
of people, goods and ideas that characterized the Atlantic world
than Ireland'.[6] Ireland's place in Atlantic history has received most
recognition for the manner in which the actions of the English
in Ireland of the 1560s and 1570s provided the template for the
subsequent English colonial enterprise of the 1600s on the other side
of the Atlantic. Links between Ireland and America solidified with
the growing immigration and trade of the eighteenth century. From
1720 to the time of the American Revolution, tens of thousands of
Presbyterian Scotch-Irish emigrated from the Ulster counties to
British North America. Irish mercantile interest expanded, extending
from the fishing of Newfoundland to trading in sugar and slaves in
the Caribbean. The influence of the Atlantic world was bi-directional.
The American Revolution, closely followed in Ireland, was critical to
the formation of the Volunteers and in the repeal of the Penal Laws.
In the 1790s, numerous United Irishmen were exiled to America (not
least Haddock's early supporter Denis Driscol), from which grew the
first consciously Irish-American communities. With its proximity to
the rich grasslands and pastoral surplus of its hinterland, even rumour
of war was a stimulus to the Cork economy, dominated as it was by
the provisions industry. During the interminable French wars, some
of the greatest convoys in maritime history gathered in Cork harbour,
sometimes for several weeks while waiting for contrary winds to settle,
before heading west to the Americas. By 1820, Ireland and the Irish
had given to America commodities, ideas and above all people.[7] To
that eclectic mix was now added Marsden Haddock and his *Androides*.

After Waterloo, Cork was in the economic doldrums. Local
newspapers copied long extracts from a manual published by the
Shamrock Society of New York, titled *Hints to emigrants from Europe*,
extolling the attractions of America:

> emphatically the best country on earth for those who will labour.
> By industry, they can earn more wages here than anywhere in
> the world. Our governments are frugal; they demand few taxes,

so that the earnings of the poor man are left to enrich himself ...
Industrious men need never lack employment in America.

Had he read the piece, the mechanic in Haddock would have approved
of the quotation from the American founding father, Benjamin
Franklin: 'God Almighty is a mechanic, the greatest in the universe'.
Some portions seemed directed at Haddock himself: 'Men of science
who can apply their knowledge to useful and practical purposes may
be very advantageously settled'.[8]

Whatever the attractions of America, push was a stronger force
than pull. If the later years of the war were trying for Cork retail
businesses, peace did not bring any relief. By 1820, a miasma of misery
hung over the city, with little sign of a turn for the better. The post-
Waterloo economic depression aggravated already endemic poverty
and unemployment. A succession of poor harvests worsened hunger
and disease. The city had just recovered from a devastating typhus
epidemic. Sectarianism and political rancour were rampant. The
south Munster area was on the verge of the worst agrarian upheaval
in sixty years, that of Captain Rock and his disciples. Provincial
England itself was in an agitated state throughout Haddock's years
of touring. The market worn out, prospects for a business such as
Haddock's were not bright.

On 9 March 1820, after a 45-day voyage from Liverpool, the
Anna Maria docked in New York. Among the thirteen passengers
disembarking were Marsden Haddock, then 61 years old, and his
39-year-old son Edward.[9]

Although there was not then a large Irish-identifying population
in America, Haddock made use of such Cork and Irish connections
as he had in New York. In his first years, in each new city Haddock
invariably introduced himself as an 'organ builder from Cork'. He
came armed 'with letters of introduction from many very respectable
people in Cork' as well as from elsewhere. The influential editor of
the *New York Evening Post* William Coleman had expected Haddock's
show to be

> one of those pleasant deceptions which are only contrived to
> amuse novices and children ... But a friend for whose judgement
> and taste we have a high respect called upon us lately for the

purpose of awakening some little interest in the welfare of the proprietor of this ingenious piece of mechanism. He said he had known Mr Haddock some years before he came to this country and could state he had been honoured by the patronage of the first circles both in England and Ireland.

A likely contender as Haddock's mentor was James Haly, who had been his neighbour at the Exchange. After also running into financial difficulties, Haly too sought solace in America, setting up as a bookseller and publisher in New York – maybe Haly's support was recompense for his winning the organ in Haddock's raffle some years before. Haly at the time was an enthusiastic advertiser in the *Evening Post*, with often more than one advertisement in each issue. Haly's premises on Broadway was the ticket-office for the *Androides*. Another potential intermediary was W.H. Creagh, another failed Cork publisher in New York. Haddock's friend Denis Driscol had also fled to America, as a political rather than an economic refugee, but had died in 1810. Haddock also had epistolatory support. According to *Hibernicus*, Haddock brought with him a reputation as 'a man of genius ... In his native city, he was highly respected' and called for support for him from 'his own countrymen'.[10]

Haddock, described as a machinist, lived in New York at 62 Spring Street.[11] His was a long-term commitment to living in America: 'this ingenious organ builder intends settling in the United States'.[12] However, that his family did not join him until the following year suggests the first was a probation period. The Haddocks eased themselves comfortably into the American way of life, even if in the first year in America he inadvertently scheduled a show for Thanksgiving, for which he pleaded ignorance and apologized.[13]

The *Androides* had their first appearance on the American continent in May 1820, at the Park Hall Auction Room, 253 Broadway. The charge for boxes was 50c. and for the gallery 25c., with children under 12 years half price – 'open this and every evening, and a day exhibition on Mondays and Thursdays'. The 4th of July of his first year in New York was graced with a show every two hours between 10a.m. and 10p.m., judged among the highlights of that year's national holiday. He closed in early August, signalled as usual by the ominous 'for ever'.[14]

He next went to Boston, where he had his greatest American success. Opening in early September 1820, the show did not close until late April the following year. Boston was to his liking and he later for a time moved his residence there.[15] Haddock had further success in Philadelphia, opening there in June 1821 (table 3).[16] It was in the city of brotherly love that his family were re-united. On 28 August 1821, the brig *Boston* sailed into New York harbour, and among those disembarking were his wife Martha, aged 64 years, and his children, Jane 40 and Marsden 24.[17] Their ages on entry to America would suggest Jane and Edward were twins.

If his touring schedule in England had been determined by the depredations of the Luddites and other upheavals, his travels around America in these early years were curtailed by the ravages of yellow fever. Fever was a summer problem. His visit to Philadelphia was prolonged by reports of fever in Baltimore, the planned next stop. The *Androides* did not finally depart until mid-November,[18] opening in Baltimore on 17 December 1824. While there, the following verse was printed in his honour.

His Figures all, from Haddock's hand,
(His genius such to Nature true)
Breathe into life, at his command,
As if Dame Nature's little crew[19]

Their stay in Baltimore was again prolonged by fear of contagion.[20] He was advised not to go south to Charleston as planned. 'He takes a northern direction for the summer and a southern tour next winter'. If planning to return to New York, the Haddocks were stymied as the yellow fever hit there as well. They sheltered in Albany where he took the opportunity to exhibit in a 'vacant room in the Capitol' for a short run.[21] Haddock finally opened the Mechanic Theatre in Charleston, South Carolina, the capital of American slavery, before Christmas 1822, to great acclaim. Haddock again enjoyed significant success. For reasons unclear, his advertising transparencies were torn down, 'designedly mutilated and injured on successive nights by evil-disposed persons'.[22]

There followed a gap in the known touring schedule, opening in New York in early October 1823, where he was 'induced to make a

Table 3. Tentative listing of Haddock's itinerary in North America

1820	May–Aug.	New York NY
1820–1	Sept.–May	Boston MA
1821	June–Nov.	Philadelphia PA
1821–2	Dec.–Mar.	Baltimore MD
1822	Sept.–Oct.	Albany NY
1822–3	Dec.–Mar.	Charleston SC
1823–4	Oct.–Apr.	New York NY
1824–5	Oct.–Jan.	Boston MA
1825	Feb.–Mar.	Salem MA
	Apr.	Newburyport MA
	May	Portsmouth NH
	July	Portland ME
		St John Newfoundland
		Halifax Nova Scotia
1826	Jan.	Providence RI
		Newport RI
	Sept.–Oct.	Montreal
		Quebec
	Nov.	Burlington VT
	Dec.	Newark NJ
1827	Jan.	New Brunswick NJ
	Mar.–May	Philadelphia PA
	July	Utica NY
	Aug.	Rochester NY
		Albany NY
	Oct.	Poughkeepsie NY
1828	Jan.–Feb.	Richmond VA
	Feb.–May	Baltimore MD
	July	New Haven CT
	Aug.	Hartford CT
1829	May	Hartford CT

second attempt'. In January 1824, Haddock was ill for a week – the exhibition was reliant on him, resuming when he had recovered. He continued to garner great praise: 'they are pleasing sensible objects and their common merit is calculated to elicit the most profound attention and wonder. There is nothing mean about them – no shuffling or trick – but sublime in the extreme. They are in my opinion without parallel'.[23]

He next gave Boston a second attempt and, in what was now a set pattern, the second was much shorter than the first visit. If

Thanksgiving was sacrosanct for Americans, Christmas was not. He gave an afternoon show on Christmas Day 1824. He next visited Salem, then the tenth largest American city, where he again drew large crowds from February to late March 1825.[24]

From now, a change in his touring pattern is apparent. With the market of large urban centres fully exploited, he now showed in smaller towns for shorter runs. He travelled up the coast from Boston, for a succession of short stays in smaller centres, venturing into Canada with visits to St Johns, Newfoundland and Halifax, Nova Scotia.[25]

In early November 1825, Haddock arrived back in Boston, where he disembarked accompanied by his wife and younger son, Marsden. Soon, he was on the sea again, taking a turn south down the coast to Rhode Island, where he spent Christmas 1825, visiting Providence and Newport.[26] With shorter stays, it is likely he modified his show. There then occurred a break in the touring schedule, while Haddock explored a new business opportunity.

MINERAL WATERS

Since time immemorial, spas had been a feature of European life. Taking the waters became popular in America after the Revolution, combining as it did its presumed health benefits, rest and recreation, and escape from summer humidity and fever, with the advantage of mingling with one's social peers. The rewards of drinking mineral water may have been exaggerated, but were certainly superior to the standard medical treatments then available. Analysis of spa water was a driving force in the development of analytic chemistry, which in time enabled the commercial production of mineral water, replicating the original in composition. The Schweppes Company, the first bottlers of carbonated water in 1783, opened a London factory in 1792. Bottled mineral water allowed the supposed therapeutic benefits to be more widely shared, and the business rapidly expanded.[27]

Haddock would have been familiar with Mallow spa, the best-known in Ireland in the eighteenth century. He exhibited on two occasions in both Bath and Bristol, and when quarantining in Albany in 1822, he likely visited nearby Saratoga Springs, the leading

American watering place. His return to Cork from London in 1800 coincided with a competitive frenzy of bottled mineral water selling in his hometown. Apothecaries, vintners, manufacturers and others shared the market: Jenning's soda-water factory making different varieties were the only producers in Cork; the vintners Farrell and Roche were the sole agents for Schweppes of London in Munster; but another vintner, Rogers, imported Schweppes through a London wholesaler, upsetting the monopoly; Haines, an apothecary, was sole agent in Cork for the Dublin manufacturer, Thwaites; Bastable, also an apothecary, claimed to be the only outlet for manufactured Cheltenham waters; and Jenning's claimed labels were taken off his mineral water bottles and put on those of inferior Dublin manufacture; while all proclaimed the superiority of their product and the support of the medical profession.[28]

For the Haddocks, mineral-water production was a commercial opportunity that hopefully was about to blossom as it had in Ireland and in England. The suspicion is that this new venture was to enable a settled life, for a couple getting older, after years of the tiresome peripatetic life of constant touring. The Haddock family, father and sons, described themselves in the 1824 New York Directory as manufacturers of mineral water at 62 Spring Street. Whether a testament to his ingenuity or to his powers of self-promotion, he claimed to have 'invented an apparatus for the manufacture of artificial mineral waters of every description', which he demonstrated before the mayor of New York. Boston had been the location of his greatest commercial success in America. To there, in June 1826, Haddock moved both his residence and the mineral-water factory, *Haddock's Soda and Artificial Mineral Water Establishment*, now located at 120 Washington Street, three doors from, appropriately, Water Street.[29]

His apparatus was 'so constructed that the carbonic acid gas from the time it is generated until received in the water does not come in contact with any deleterious metal whatsoever, as it passes into the machine through silver apertures and silver cocks'. 'Persons who drink the saline waters such as Rochelle &c. will find this the most pleasing and efficacious – as they are impregnated immediately from the machine'. The waters he provided were Soda Pyrmont, Seltzer, Rochelle, Cheltenham, Epsom and plain acidulous. His mineral

4. Haddock bottle from *c*.1826

waters were supplied in bottles also, as well as bottled Congress water from Saratoga, fresh from the springs. The Haddock bottles, by modern historians regarded as primitive, were manufactured in the mid-1820s and have been found in New York City, Boston and Hartford (fig. 4). The manufacturer may have been the Coventry Glass Works in New Hampshire.[30]

He was even more ambitious. To complement his new range of mineral waters, he opened Mr Haddock's *Retreat for the Ladies* in Boston Broadway: 'He who has pleased them with his *Androides*, perplexed with his ingenuity, can also please them with his Soda and perplex them with his contrivance. The Retreat is in the second storey, perfectly retired, yet airy and pleasant'. 'The Ladies and Gentlemen of Boston are respectfully informed that his room is fitted up for the exclusive sale of Artificial Mineral Waters, and as no Spiritous Liquors of any kind are sold, he hopes the Ladies will honour the establishment with their patronage'.[31]

His best-laid plans were not to come to fruition. Tragedy intervened. In the summer of 1826, Haddock's wife, Martha, died after a short illness, aged 74 years. 'She joined in prayer the day before, and could see to read and work at her needle without spectacles a fortnight before she died'.[32] Martha's death altered his plans – his new venture did not continue, maybe suggesting its primary purpose was indeed to facilitate a more settled routine.

After an appropriate interval, touring resumed. Sea voyages were not always pleasant and from now he began to travel more on the internal waterways. He won 'high encomiums' in Montreal, and went next to Quebec. On the return route, he exhibited in Burlington,

Vermont, on Lake Champlain and quite likely in other locations on this sortie into the interior. He travelled on to New Jersey and, some weeks later, he paid his second visit to Philadelphia, five years after his first, the second visit again shorter than the first.[33] In the summer and autumn of 1827, he made another incursion inland, travelling along the Hudson River and the recently constructed Erie Canal, re-visiting Albany as well as several other smaller centres. Early the following year, he took another turn south, again avoiding the pestilential summer. After several weeks in Richmond, he paid a second visit to Baltimore.[34]

Although some gaps in his schedule may be accounted for by a dearth of sources, the intensity of his touring seems to have reduced. He appeared in New Haven, Connecticut, in the summer of 1828. Organ work there delayed his arrival in Hartford, which he likely reached by the navigable Connecticut River. He exhibited in Hartford both in September 1828 and after a long gap again in May 1829, which were his last appearances with the *Androides*. In his later touring, the admittance charge had fallen to 25c. The pieces he exhibited were the staples of a long career: the Spelling Automaton, Fruitery, Liquor Merchant, Telegraph and Highland Oracle.[35] Haddock seemingly had inexhaustible energy. He did not rest. Most gaps in his schedule are explained by further extra-curricular activities, and at least some of the interludes were accounted for by forays into the theatre world.

THEATRE

The Haddock family were in the business of creating illusions. Although the pieces were admired for what they did rather than how they looked, they were possessed of some grace and were not without beauty. They occupied the overlap of the artisan and artist, between utility and art. His creations were often considered works of art and Haddock an artist: 'The approximation to intelligence, volition and action which these little wooden figures display, prove the perfection of which art is capable'.[36]

The artistry of the Haddocks did not confine itself to mechanical figures. The much-admired transparencies that Haddock showed in the late 1790s were created by the young John Corbet, who had lived with him in London for a time. There was also artistic talent in the Haddock family however. His younger son Marsden, at this time in his late twenties, was a talented artist as well as being a scene-painter. He often collaborated with his father in creating illusions on stage. In April 1826, the Boston Theatre produced *Cherry and Fair Star; or, The Children of Cyprus*, a magical tale of a prince and princess, under sentence of death, shipwrecked on a desert island. The scene painting in particular was much-praised: 'a new scene painted by Mr Haddock, artist of the Boston Theatre ... being a view of the celebrated Pass of Missolonghi ... may be justly ranked among the first and most effective scenes we have ever witnessed in the Boston Theatre. We hope that Mr Haddock will long continue among us'. Vivid stage representations of dramatic scenes with light and sound effects were popular, none more so than shipwrecks, a constant in the Atlantic world. The older Haddock in this production made his contribution to the death-throes of the doomed ship – the machinery was by 'Mr Haddock'.[37] The theatres in Boston and Providence were parts of the one commercial concern. In May–June 1826, in another gap in the touring schedule, in Providence, Rhode Island, not alone did the younger Haddock provide the scenery for the first production of the season, *William Tell*, but 'Mr Haddock the artist also painted and decorated the interior of the Theatre'.[38]

Stricken vessels were a Haddock speciality. In May 1827, in the New York Theatre in the Bowery, the Haddocks had another opportunity to create the illusion of a storm-tossed ship, in a production of *The Flying Dutchman; or, Phantom Ship*. The younger Marsden Haddock was one of the scene-painters and the machinery again was constructed by the older Haddock.[39]

Their travels on the inland waterways were not wasted hours. Back in the Bowery two years later, during the opening performance of the season was shown a diorama of the 'splendid and unrivalled scenery of the Hudson' – the painting was by the younger Haddock and 'the steam-boats and other mechanical and moving objects' by the older. The entertainment gave a narrative of a trip along the interior rivers and canals: 'by stationary boat and moving diorama, it carried the characters from the wharf in New York and up the Hudson – with accompanying storm, fog etc. – to the Catskills by moonlight, Albany, the Erie Canal and Niagara'.[40]

PAPER MANUFACTURE

Haddock, versatile and indefatigable, was irrepressible. Not discouraged by his previous experiences in Cork, in another venture in America he resurrected his interest in paper manufacture. That he had exhibited before the RDS paper of his own novel manufacture was a staple of his promotional material in Britain and in America.[41] Possibly, he took greater interest in paper production after his mineral-water business had failed; his interest in paper reached a culmination in 1827–8.

That he was involved in experiments in paper manufacture was integrated into his advertising material. In Philadelphia, working models were to be seen every evening at his performance.[42] In Baltimore, he was 'delayed in completing two miniature models for useful manufactories, which he is inventing; one is finished, and the other will be completed in a few days – when he will set off for Washington to obtain patents'.[43]

The process was similar to the one he had developed in Cork on his return from London twenty-five years before. On this occasion, the patent was granted, on 17 June 1828, in which his residence was given as New York.[44] 'In the model deposited in the patent office ... the motions appear to be well performed, by means which are both ingenious and simple'.[45]

Why he had lingered so long in Hartford, Connecticut, his last appearance with the *Androides*, was to further develop the industrial application of his newly patented invention.

> Mr Haddock's patented machine for the manufacture of paper in sheets, upon the dipping process, was put in operation last October [1829], at Messrs Seymour & Copeland's Manufactory, in Hartford, where it was made under Mr Haddock's inspection. There was some paper pulp produced from a mill, and the machine operated upon in presence of a number of respectable paper manufacturers, and other gentlemen of science, and was by all highly approved of. This machine possesses a property, among others, that it can make laid as well as woven paper, as it undergoes all the movements of vatman and coucher, and makes six sheets cap paper, at a dip; and is said to be a saving

of a thousand dollars a year – it doing the work of two vats in twelve hours, besides making an article sure to meet a market. The patent is in possession of Messrs Robinson and Barber, of Hartford, and it is much to be regretted that an invention of that magnitude has not been brought forward long ere this, by those gentlemen or Mr Haddock.[46]

Alas, history has relegated Haddock to the list of the less-noted patentees in the history of paper-making in America.[47] It is here, in Hartford, Connecticut, that we lose track of Marsden Haddock. Possibly, the success of his last enterprise enabled him to comfortably retire. It was about this time that his youngest son died, the news reaching his native city in July 1829: 'at Albany, North America, Mr Marsden Warren Haddock, formerly of Cork' an artist of very considerable talents.'[48] Where Marsden senior thereafter lived, and died, we have no information. *Haddock's Exhibition of Androides; or, Wonderful imitations of human nature* seems not to have performed again.

TOURING

Haddock's touring circuit was the English-speaking Atlantic world, Ireland and Britain and its former American colonies. 'On account of the labour and care requisite in moving the pieces ... Mr Haddock can exhibit them only in places where it is probable that he will meet with liberal encouragement'.[49] The greatest population densities and the best transport options were to be found on the Atlantic littoral. His preference was for large urban areas, his travels hugging the coastlines on both sides of the English-speaking Atlantic.

Haddock's career trajectory followed the popularity of shows and exhibitions – early success followed by decline. Mechanical exhibitions, as well as the freak shows, panoramas, wax works and sundry assorted entertainments initially rode the crest of a wave, but losing the ability to amaze and perplex, the wave broke on the shore. The quest for novelty, the lure of new attractions and advances in the spread of popular education and literacy, all served to reduce credulity and the capacity for wonder, making it harder to attract audiences.

Remarkably, the format of Haddock's show remained essentially unchanged from Cork in 1794 to his last appearance in Hartford, Connecticut in 1829 – he ended with what he started with. Greater competition in cosmopolitan London obliged him to add new pieces likely not of his own creation, such as the writing automaton and other figures. Such innovation was not necessary if showing to new audiences not previously exposed. His touring was a prolonged search for the naïve and the gullible, ever seeking the uninitiated. As metropolitan London was drained of possibilities, the search for the easily impressed necessitated him pushing into the provinces to ever smaller towns. After exhausting the market in Britain, the same pattern repeated itself in America, early success followed by diminishing returns for ever greater efforts.

As his entertainment remained constant in format over three decades, so also did it scarcely change as he travelled through Ireland, Britain and North America. Haddock liked to add local colour to his entertainment. He often created make-believe topical narratives involving the *Androides* as a promotional device. In Dublin, a Collector for the window- and hearth-money called at the little Fruitess's house. The *Androides* refused to pay. The Collector, proceeding to distrain, was opposed by the porter of the house and the dog, while being pelted with oranges by the Fruitress. While the Collector tried to make his escape, the little sweep flung soot in his eye. The Liquor Merchant and the Water Pumper, alerted by telegraphic dispatch, threw water on the soot-covered Collector, giving 'a very pleasing contour to the poor Collector's countenance'.[50] Whereas in London, the names of the conquering admirals were inscribed by the Writing Automaton, nearly thirty years later in Massachusetts the Spelling automaton was giving the audience 'John Quincy Adams'.[51] However, other than these superficial accommodations to locality, it is notable how little necessity there was for Haddock to alter his show or to make compromises to entertain different audiences. An increasing uniformity of urban culture facilitated his touring across the English-speaking world. This ready acceptance of his entertainment required little or no concessions by Haddock. Urban popular entertainment differed little between London and Cork (even if the latter was some years behind on the touring circuit). Britain or more specifically London had maintained a firm grip on American culture after the

Revolution and for long after – continued cultural domination some recompense for military defeat. Popular London entertainments promptly re-emerged with little change in format in the former colonies. This cultural homogeneity facilitated a near-seamless transfer of entertainments such as Haddock's across the Atlantic.

The *Androides* on-tour was a mobile, self-contained family concern. Except that Corbet lived with Haddock in Norfolk Street off the Strand and his daughter accompanied him to Limerick in 1810, there is no information as to his companions when exhibiting in Ireland and Britain. In America, Haddock and his son Edward arrived first. When the family re-united, usually three members travelled: when they arrived in Charleston in November 1822 on board the *Camillus* from New York, both sons accompanied him;[52] and when returning to Boston from Halifax in November 1825, his wife Martha and son Marsden were his companions.[53] They travelled light. On the sloop *Hannah Ann* from Baltimore to Philadelphia, six boxes were sufficient for the *Androides* and their belongings.[54] In Britain, coach-roads were the likely mode of transport, but canals might have been used also. In America, the Haddocks travelled on water. They made use of the coastal routes from Charleston, South Carolina, in the south to St Johns, Newfoundland, in the north. Towns in the interior they also reached by water – the Hudson–Lake Champlain–St Laurence waterways to Montreal and Quebec and the recently constructed Erie Canal for several towns on its route.

'The attention which has been paid to the comfort of the audience by the accommodating manner and taste with which the Theatre is fitted up is highly praiseworthy'. Haddock's was a 'Theatre in miniature'.[55] Audience size was hampered by the size of the exhibits. While the automatons were three foot in size, the assemblages were smaller, the Telegraph only a foot high. The necessity to have close-up seats to appreciate the figures limited attendance, precluding large crowds. All the venues used were small throughout his exhibiting career.[56] Advice that 'as theatre is small, it is absolutely necessary that servants are sent timely to keep places' was a constant refrain in Britain and in Ireland,[57] but not in egalitarian America. 'The room is fitting up as a theatre, with boxes &c. in a peculiar style'.[58] Despite tiered seating and boxes, careful arrangement was not always possible. In Albany in 1822, Haddock had to make do with a 'vacant room in the Capitol'.[59] In Charleston, Haddock hoped 'the ladies ... will not be offended at his requesting their not wearing bonnets in his room, it being small and does not admit of sufficient elevation'.[60] He cared for his clientele in the extremes of weather. A good fire for the patrons was maintained in winter.[61] In another example of his ingenuity, to manage the heat of the American summer, he constructed what he called a retro-grade fan, 'a great luxury during these warm evenings'.[62]

> A lady's lap-dog, resting its two fore-feet on the front rail of the boxes, seemed as happy as if he enjoyed the entertainment; this was all well till the Fruitery was introduced, when the little Machine Dog began to bark, which so irritated the lady's dog, that barking between the two dogs commenced with rapid response, and laughter of course ensued so as to suspend the exhibition for many minutes; the Machine Dog was however the conqueror, as the lady's dog hung its tail and went off quite disconcerted.[63]

Most mechanical exhibitions had a fixed repertoire, with the same repetitive sequence of movements in every performance. Haddock's distinguishing attraction was audience participation and interaction: 'To converse with mechanical images, and to be delighted with their intelligence, is a novelty which cannot fail to please and astonish'. As well as barking dogs, most of his pieces responded to questions and requests: 'These figures without any connection to machinery performed the commands of any person in the room'.[64] This quality encouraged repeat attendance for even the jaded: 'As acting at the will of the company, each exhibition of these extraordinary figures must be materially different from the other' and 'the pleasure of seeing them is increased on the repetition'.[65]

The years straddling the turn of the eighteenth century are designated the age of revolutions, but the turmoil affected much more than the great affairs of nations and empires. 'Give me something to desire' pleaded a fictional character of Dr Johnson's, highlighting another revolutionary change of the period: an explosion in consumerism matched by a similar transformation in its accomplice, advertising – both seeking to satisfy the unrelenting 'pursuit of happiness'. Haddock pitched himself into the advertising fray with gusto.[66]

A glance at the sources for this work will indicate the central role of newspaper advertising in the promotion of his show. Haddock was an energetic purchaser of advertising space in local newspapers, and, probably not unrelated, garnered much editorial attention, uniformly positive, often extravagantly so. As 'few [sources] are more engagingly disingenuous or downright mendacious than show-business publicity', these must be treated with caution.[67] The planted items and puff-pieces were full of hyperbole and elaborate language, with regular declarations of being favoured by nobility, gentry and even royalty. Haddock was adept at public relations and manipulation. Being such a prolific advertiser, he was rewarded with regular acclaim in newspaper editorials and placed *puff* items in news columns. The same anecdotes and exaggerated claims are repeated ad nauseum. His departure was always ominously looming, and he was forever being called away elsewhere to create new ingenious inventions. As in Newburyport, Massachusetts, it is likely that many of the adulatory letters published about the *Androides* were from Haddock's own hand. An innocent promotional feature was regular elaborate make-believe stories of supposed quarrels between Haddock's various figures, a regular feature in Ireland and Britain.[68] Some of his grandiose claims verged on the mendacious. It was unlikely the emperor of Russia made secret overtures to Haddock to purchase the Liquor Merchant in London in 1798 and even less likely he would try again twenty years later.[69]

Wide circulation though they had, newspapers did not have a universal reach. Haddock was resourceful and innovative in other key forms of advertising. He regularly published handbills, effective in the local market in a face-to-face world. Ephemeral as they are, only those from London, Glasgow and Norwich are extant.[70] Many Dublin handbills from the period are illustrated with startling imagery of the whole spectrum of popular entertainment,[71] but unfortunately Haddock's contain only a simple graphic of the Telegraph machine. There is no other known pictorial representation of his automatons or assemblages extant. When he recommended touring in 1810, Haddock used the less common device of a published pamphlet, part promotional, part explanatory and part entertainment (fig. 5). The first was printed by his neighbour on Castle Street, William West.[72] As well as the original Cork version, there are editions extant from

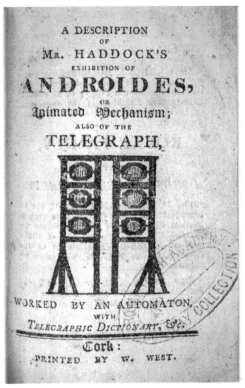

5. Title page of Haddock's promotional booklet,
first published in Cork in 1810 (RIA)

Dublin, Newcastle-on-Tyne and Bristol, all with the same content.
In these, Haddock could revel in his fondness for mediocre verse.

While the elite were the optimum customers, the non-elite were
of incomparably greater number. Many were not fully literate and it
is likely that many of these became aware of advertisements by having
the contents read to them. This group included many of the middling
sort who had discretionary money to spend, putting a premium on
non-print advertising. It is likely Haddock employed street-criers,
portable hand-signs, and even drummers to drum up business. In
both London and America, Haddock deployed transparencies, the
equivalent of modern neon-lit billboards, not a common ploy at the
time. Even the prominence of his name on his mineral-water bottles
was intentional and calculated. Also of promotional value, to his
credit, Haddock frequently, usually as he was departing, donated

proceeds of shows to local charities, for example in Belfast, New York, Boston and Salem.[73]

Even at the dawn of modern advertising there were complaints of saturation coverage. 'Whatever is common is despised', complained Dr Johnson in the mid-eighteenth century. Rhetorical flourishes and hyperbole lost their punch when everyone else was deploying similarly exaggerated claims. True novelty was the optimum promotional feature. The freshness of his entertainment worked to Haddock's advantage in his early years, particularly in America, but the increasing competition in automaton exhibition inexorably pushed him into ever smaller centres.[74]

Haddock tended not to use his nationality as a promotional ploy: it would have been less useful in the years before the great migrations that began after Waterloo; also, anti-Irishness was prevalent in both Britain and America at the time. He described himself as 'a mechanic of the Irish soil' in Dublin and in Belfast, but not when touring elsewhere.[75] Except for some Irish melodies on the organ, there was little distinctively Irish about the entertainment. If anything, in such as the Highland Oracle, Scottish influence was more apparent, driven by the frenzy for all things Scottish at the time Walter Scott was at the zenith of his fame.

With its tendency to compartmentalize, analysis of the entertainment industry can obscure as much as it reveals. Ultimately, motivations were simple. As regards the audience, popular and other entertainment should be seen simply as a source of pleasure, satisfying the impulses for new experiences, amusement, spectacle and excitement. Attendance allowed the exercise of imagination and wonder, fulfilled the need for novelty and, not least, was a diversion from the often-mundane reality of stolid urban life. For the operators and performers, popular entertainment was, above all, a commercial venture, and the pursuit of profit provided little space for other agendas.[76] There was money to be made. Haddock made no secret of his own motivations.

> Here Haddock still his friends to please
> Consults their pleasure, health and ease
> But ask him, why he takes such pains?
> He whispers for his private gains[77]

At the peak of their popularity, the *Androides* was a lucrative business. The four-year residency in London would have been the high-water mark of his income and likely provided the money for later misplaced investments. By the end of his nine-month residency in Boston, a reported 16,000 had attended.[78] He donated $92, two days receipts without expenses deducted, in support of the local Asylum for Indigent Boys.[79] With income such as this, Haddock must have accumulated significant amounts during busy runs.

Haddock charged what the market could bear. In both London and Charleston, he chanced doubling his usual admission charge, a strategy he quickly abandoned.[80] On one occasion in Cork he declared he would not reduce his admission charge approaching the end of the run, implying such was his usual practice. In his final years in America, the admission had fallen to 25*c.*, which with short runs and increased travelling expenses must have represented a significant fall in income.[81]

When busy, he had a morning and an evening show daily and, when less so, an evening show only. He was always happy to oblige the clientele – he arranged early morning shows to suit the race goers of York and the farming community in East Anglia,[82] and after-school shows for London schoolchildren. He was similarly eager to accommodate private viewings: in London, 'a party of six or more may have one, at their own hour, by giving a previous notice'; in Montreal, 'day exhibitions to select parties by giving timely notice'; and in Rochester, New York, 'private viewing for those who take 10 dollars or upwards in tickets and giving three- or four-hours' notice'.[83]

Then, as now, newspaper reporting of the entertainment industry is notoriously unreliable. However, the laudatory remarks on Haddock's personal attributes are conspicuous by their constancy, and even more marked in America: 'to the manners of a gentleman, he unites those feelings of modesty and reserve which always characterise true merit'; 'a gentleman of so much private worth and professional excellence'; 'irreproachable character and gentlemanly deportment' and many more such. 'Mr Haddock's genteel and unassuming manner forms a part of the pleasure of the evening's entertainment'. His showmanship, his elegant manner and that he was equally cheerful before a sparsely attended as a full house suggests that the show's popularity was reliant not solely on technology. Rather his personability and urbanity were major components of the enjoyment and success of the show.[84]

Personable and urbane as he may have been, he was not without a deal of pride. Haddock never considered himself a mere entertainer or exhibitor: 'Haddock, not professionally an exhibitor and has other concerns to attend to, may leave town in a few days'. He was variously described in advertising as 'that celebrated mechanic', 'one of the greatest mechanics of the age' and 'one of the first mechanics of the age'. The appellation must have been to his liking as the venue wherever he was appearing was re-named the Mechanic Theatre. Whether accurately or not, he styled himself 'inventor of the *Androides*'.[85] That he was 'professionally an organ builder' was emphasized in his advertising throughout his career. When Haddock announced his intention of settling in London 'in this great metropolis ... [he was] determined to exert himself as an organ builder and machinist to the utmost of his abilities to bring forward inventions, both useful and entertaining'.[86] He was of more substance than a mere entertainer. It was as if the frivolity of the *Androides* was pulling him away from more serious work: 'his other concerns (as he is not professionally an exhibiter) might call him to New York, where he is intent on carrying on some ingenious manufacture'.[87]

Haddock took pains to distinguish himself from lower forms of entertainment. 'Here it is that the admirers of true genius may feast their intellect, without being obliged to hear theatrical tales of ribaldry, which too often terminate in farce'.[88] In Newburyport, Massachusetts, in 1825, an editorial insert thought to be 'from the facile and exultant pen of Mr Haddock' stated that

> there are so many paltry Exhibitions [that] visit this and other towns, that the public are inclined to think that the *Androides* partake of the puppet show or something of a low stamp, but those who have visited this exhibition are of a different opinion, and pronounce it to be the greatest and most wonderful production of human invention that ever appeared in any age or nation.[89]

In Baltimore in 1828, it was proclaimed the 'Automatons don't partake of the puppet show, nor any juggling tricks to impose upon the vulgar'.[90] He would be disappointed that in histories of the stage he is usually relegated to the columns describing those very entertainments 'of a low stamp' that he was so anxious not to be associated with.[91]

Haddock's exhibition offered more than mere amusement and diversion. In addition to entertainment value, attendance carried a promise of instruction and stimulation: 'no public place can be better calculated to please and instruct young minds'.[92] Haddock's show had obvious appeal to the young and impressionable: 'we have witnessed the innocent wonder and gratification excited in the juvenile part of his audiences'.[93] A frequent refrain was that, inspired by experiencing Haddock's show, nascent abilities were stirred – who knew what 'dormant genius may be roused to produce most curious and useful works'?[94] He pursued their attendance, with half-price admission, scheduling after-school shows and often reserving front-row seats for his younger clientele.[95] He deliberately teased the audience to discover the mechanism behind his seemingly autonomous *Androides*:

> the master movement by which the automata appear to reason, calculate, see and execute with promptitude and exactness, is so scientifically concealed, as to afford a full exercise for the judgement of the mature and profound.[96]

Social class distinction was also at issue here – whereas the lower orders were happy to be diverted for a time, the upper classes preferred their entertainment with a dusting of instruction. Be it Haddock's *Androides*, exhibits from exotic Australia or mechanical orreries explaining astronomical phenomena, this merging of entertainment with intellectual stimulation made for perfect Enlightenment recreation.

Through pricing and promotion, Haddock pursued the elite and the monied. In Ireland, he attracted a 'crowded fashionable audience'; in provincial England an 'assemblage of rank and fashion'; in London, advertising was trained on 'the Nobility and gentry'; and in America he appealed 'to a polite and discerning audience'.[97] However, class distinctions in popular entertainment were lessening. While admission fees had an inevitable influence on the make-up of the audience, relish for entertainment transcended class: the *Androides* did not appeal exclusively to either rich or poor. On both sides of the Atlantic, 'the attention of the people of every class was drawn towards it'.[98] His prices, while not cheap, were not extravagant. While Haddock may have directed his advertising at the elite, he was more than happy to admit the middling sort and the aspiring artisan classes. Novel and original entertainments and other cultural activities usually originated in cities and first attracted a select, urban audience. However, such new ventures tended to quickly trickle down through the middling and artisan classes and in time throughout the urban system. The upper-class elite was often the portal by which entertainments gained traction among lower socio-economic classes.[99] After Haddock had departed London, the *Androides* appeared in variety shows, aimed at a lower grade of customer.

In Cork, as elsewhere, there was an ambivalence about social class and one's place in the world. In 1802,

> a one-shilling gallery is about to be added to the accommodations of the theatre ... we do most warmly approve of opening so rational and so moral a source of entertainment to the humbler orders ... The recreations of the theatre are no indifferent substitution for the libations of the whiskey shop. ... It is a very unwarrantable squeamishness which presumes that a poor man at Cork is worse conducted and less fit to be the inmate of a public place than the disorderly rabble of Dublin and London.

However, confidence in the public demeanour of the Cork proletariat was not complete, as the editorial concluded with: 'a strong recommendation that the proper number of Peace Officers be stationed thro' the House'.[100]

Cork and its hinterland were Gaelicized to a greater extent than other Irish urban centres, including Dublin. With each economic crisis in rural Ireland, there was a fresh infusion of Irish-speakers into the warren of cabins in the north and south suburbs overlooking the River Lee. Hearing so much Irish spoken on visiting Cork in 1815, Edward Wakefield imagined he was in a foreign country. It was claimed there was more Irish spoken in London, the favourite migration destination of Cork's economically destitute in the early nineteenth century, than there was in Dublin. The popular culture of the lower orders in urban Cork is not well documented. Those activities that disturbed prevailing notions of decorum, in particular any infringement of the sanctity of the Sabbath, were those most likely to gain public attention. Pastimes such as bowl-playing on a Sunday, bull-baiting and cock-fighting or the internecine warfare between the butchers of Fair-Hill and the weavers of Blackpool were regularly denounced in the Cork newspapers (in one season's faction fighting, tomahawks imported from American culture were the weapons of choice).[101] Cork city was residentially, socially and culturally segregated. There is no evidence that the urban proletariat, the great mass of Cork's population, influenced or was ever exposed to Haddock's *Androide* entertainment. Although originating in Cork, his entertainment was divorced from the local community and the prevailing local culture.

Conclusion

'WE MIGHT ALMOST PRESUME ... A SUPERNATURAL AGENCY'

Haddock had issues to contend with that did not apply to other forms of entertainment or exhibition. Alexander Hamilton, now better known for the eponymous musical than as a founding father of the American republic, established the *New York Evening Post*. He appointed William Coleman as its inaugural editor. The controversialist Coleman was much feared, both for his acerbic pen and for his reputation as a lethal duellist. Soon after Haddock's arrival in New York, Coleman wrote a piece that was interpreted by some to mean 'Haddock ... like a second Prometheus with wicked art [had] created "men"'.[1] Recently arrived in America, the publicity generated would not have done Haddock any harm. However, the controversy underlines an issue that was operative throughout Haddock's exhibiting career: the more human-like he made his creations, the more apparently inexplicable their actions, the more potentially unsettling was the effect on the audience.

Haddock would have considered himself a product of the Enlightenment. Even though they were perceived as mere entertainment, he was proud of the ingenuity of his pieces and the potential practical application of the mechanics involved. But he lived in turbulent times. The French Revolution and the Terror, followed by the prolonged Napoleonic wars, destabilized the world order. Occurring at the height of dominance of the Age of Reason, these near-apocalyptic events caused many to turn away from the rationality of the previous decades. In the uncertainty of the new Romantic Age, the automaton became increasingly associated with the magical and supernatural rather than as exemplars of the mechanical art.[2]

Prometheus, who moulded mortal man out of clay, was a constant in descriptions of the *Androides*. 'The artist seems to have bestowed on his figures the Promethean fire, for they display, in a manner almost exceeding belief, the rational powers and faculties of man'.[3]

Their capacity to perturb was a reflection of the sophistication of the audience. In our knowing world, it is difficult to appreciate the sensations of wonder and awe Haddock's pieces produced. For some, these sensations were a part of their attraction, but for others their response merged into uncertainty and dread. For the many that believed in the power of some to harness otherworldly powers, magic was a plausible explanation of such phenomena, magic that came from demoniacal or satanic sources. The *Androides* were unworldly objects and Haddock a modern-day sorcerer. The more convincingly life-like were the mechanical pieces and the greater their encroachment into notions of what makes us human, the more disconcerting the effect of automatons and other figures.

Such considerations were on display from the beginnings of his career. According to the deist Denis Driscol, Cork's most outspoken opponent of organized religion,

> the days of prejudice and superstition are not yet passed away! The efforts of our ingenious townsman have been mistaken for enchantment, but in the present century no person has suffered for witchcraft, else poor Haddock would certainly be burnt as a magician, such extraordinary effects have his astonishing machines produced.[4]

In Liverpool, the impression made was such that it '[is] well for Mr Haddock that he does not exhibit his wonderful *Androides* in a country where the Inquisition exists, as he would certainly be suspected of dealing in the *Black art* and fall a sacrifice to superstition'.[5] The great Jaquet-Droz, accused of heresy, had been indeed imprisoned by the Spanish Inquisition.[6]

With the expanding sway of religion and respectability in society, Haddock went to some lengths to deny any moral or religious irregularity in his entertainment, to downplay any sinister connotations. That his show 'cannot possibly offend against any moral or religious scruples of the most fastidious' was an invariable in his advertising in Ireland, Britain and America.[7] In England, Haddock trumpeted the support of those deemed the epitome of rectitude:

> Even the grave and solemn people called the Quakers are in numbers attracted to this ingenious rational performance. Hence,

we may infer that all ranks and descriptions of the community consider this exhibition as strictly moral and excellent in its kind.[8]

Frivolous or irregular entertainment was discouraged during the solemnity of Lent, while that of an instructive nature was permitted. Haddock ensured he was on the right side of that virtuous demarcation line, begging 'permission to acquaint the nobility and gentry that his (moral) exhibition of *Androides* will be presented every day during Lent'.[9] Concern about the *dark arts* may have been a greater issue in America, as he spent much time in puritan New England. While exhibiting in Salem, Massachusetts, of witch-trial notoriety, he willingly discontinued Saturday-evening shows as they were not in 'accord with a custom of long standing in this town'.[10]

One of the most famed automatons was the Chess Player, which, while exhibiting in America, was often considered a rival to Haddock. Dressed as a malevolent Turk, the Chess Player was presented as a figure of darkness, with supernatural and sinister undertones. Its ability to beat all-comers in chess added to the sense of ominous menace. In contrast, Haddock made his show as non-threatening as possible, designed to entertain rather than to unsettle or frighten: 'Mr Haddock ... makes no secret of the fact that he controls the movements of the Automaton himself by a mechanical power, the only secret in the exhibition being the means of communicating his will to the machine'.[11]

There is no mystery as to how the automatons, the programmed writing and spelling figures functioned, but there is less clarity about the other figures and assemblages. No machine to then invented could provide answers, verbal or signalled, to arbitrary questions. If we take it the *Androides* were not supernaturally endowed, we must try to explain their mechanism of action.

Great care was taken to set up the stage and auditorium to his own specification, requiring several days of preparation. 'The completeness of the machinery is so great that Mr Haddock will have been occupied nearly a fortnight in putting it together before he can exhibit it'.[12] There is a suspicion that such careful preparation was at least in part an exercise in perfecting subterfuge.

The organ and its music were a central part of Haddock's entertainment. At the beginning of the show, the maestro himself played melodies on the table organ, an instrument of his own creation and construction.

> All these figures and the machinery connected with them are placed upon a table in the centre of the room, covered on the top with green cloth, apparently for the purpose of excluding all suspicion of any possible communication with the moving images. The table is in fact an organ, the interior of which is exposed to view, by turning over the top where you can discover nothing but windpipes and other appendages to the musical instrument. After the performance on the organ is finished, the top is replaced and the exhibition commences.

All further organ music during interludes as each piece was removed came from the self-playing barrel organ. The table organ lay apparently redundant for the remainder of the performance, serving only as a platform for display of the pieces.

This ostentatious exposure of the innards of this organ, before it was again concealed, is reminiscent of the subterfuge associated with that most famed automaton, the Chess Player. To a much greater degree than Haddock's, there was endless scrutiny and debate of its inner workings, Edgar Allan Poe being one of many obsessed with its mechanism. Many saw parallels between Haddock's assemblages and the sinister Turk. 'The secret means by which the celebrated automaton chess player appears to be governed by an immediate intelligence and which have baffled the penetration of the most ingenious mechanics, seem to have been discovered by Mr Haddock'.[13]

> That they [the *Androides*] all proceed from voluntary motion is undoubted, but in what manner this is communicated to the figure, evades the conjecture of the most acute; and I venture to say that when it shall be found out how the automaton corresponds with his telegraph, then will the secret of the celebrated chess automaton, which has so long perplexed, and still perplexes, the most ingenious philosophers in Europe, be brought to light.[14]

The secrets of the chess-playing Turk were indeed ultimately exposed to the light. The figure was operated by a skilled chess-player, concealed within the figure's mechanism, placed there *after* a similarly ostentatious inspection had been offered to the audience. What many had suspected – that the activity of the *Androides* was 'effected by means of machinery which is concealed from view'[15] and by a 'secreted confederate'[16] – was almost certainly true.[17] The likelihood is that access to the performing pieces by the concealed assistant was through the table organ with the innards removed. The concealed assistant must have had mathematical skills, mental agility and manual dexterity of a high order, given the rapidity with which he solved arithmetical conundrums for the Oracle and chose the correct signals for the Telegraph. It is significant both that the first two pieces displayed in the performance were the automatons, thereby providing time for the subterfuge to be perfected, and that after Haddock played the table organ, the instrument was idle for the rest of the performance. It is likely that the strings furiously pulled by the Telegraph's hand were not those that moved the shutters.

It is fitting that the organ should have been so intrinsic to the mechanism of the *Androides*. Throughout his working life, the musical organ was central to Haddock's activities. He was particularly proud of the table organ he claimed to have invented and constructed.[18] Haddock did not engage as much with the organ business in America. He made no known attempt to make or sell the instrument. However, the instrument always remained an integral part of the entertainment. He opened with the table organ and used the barrel organ throughout. When opportunity arose for further organ work, he did not let the occasion pass. He was delayed going to Hartford, Connecticut, the location of his final performance, as he was repairing the organs in both the Episcopal and Presbyterian churches in New Haven in the same state.[19]

* * *

The swelling cities of the Middle Ages were prone to fire, plague and civil strife. Large mechanical clocks were an effort to impose order and regulation (or, as some would claim, control and subjugation). These public timepieces became more elaborate with time, often ornamented with mechanically moving figures, controlled and coordinated by the clock movement. Many are regarded as masterpieces of art and of engineering. From these public pieces, automatons for entertainment emerged.

Despite their purpose to amuse and give delight, the exquisite automatons of the eighteenth century created for royalty and the nobility were more than mere frivolity. Automatons could draw, write, play music and even apparently play chess. The principles underlying their mechanisms were readily transferrable, and the same craftmanship, intricacy and ingenuity displayed could be similarly applied for utilitarian ends. Always obedient and reliable, they were functional and stable irrespective of changes in the environment.

> They have the intelligence of at least some of our species, are more economically sustained, and are moreover always ready for their work; for, as Mr Whitbread, we believe, said in justifying the preference given to machinery in England over men 'machines never play and never get drunk'.[20]

Many of the automaton pioneers made contributions to industrial mechanization. The French inventor Jacques de Vaucanson created the first completely automated loom in 1745, which pioneered the use of punch cards to automate pattern control. Pierre Jaquet-Droz himself made contributions to industrial automation. Wolfgang von Kempelen's 'Turk' chess-player inspired Edmund Cartwright to create the power loom.[21]

Some saw this technical virtuosity as a threat. Although designed for entertainment, it was a small step to design for replacement. This fear of redundancy was a growing concern as the Industrial Revolution was gathering pace. In the textile industries of Nottinghamshire, Lancashire and Yorkshire, during high unemployment in 1811 and 1812, the Luddites rose in violent protest, automated textile machinery their prime target. It has been suggested that Haddock's movements through England might have been influenced or determined by the Luddite agitation and its suppression. However, it is unlikely that the *Androides* would have been a Luddite target. If anything, it was more likely that the informed scrutiny of a discerning audience would have been even more appreciative of his skill and ingenuity. As the nineteenth century went on, automatons began to shed their associations with entertainment. The inventiveness displayed in the creation of mechanical devices was transferred to industry, the principles reappearing in the mechanisms of spinning-machines, steam-engines and other technologies.

Most popular entertainments arrived in Haddock's homeplace only after the clientele of more lucrative centres had been fully exploited. There is an irony in Cork city being the birthplace of an entertainment such as the *Androides*, there being in Haddock's time few places more disordered and unregulated. The city's beauty and charm owed more to nature than to human interference. Municipal authority was controlled by a clique that excluded most Protestants and all Catholics and, until municipal reform in the 1840s, was at constant odds with most of the populace. The population was fractured and fractious, Cork being tightly segregated along near-contiguous religious, cultural and socio-economic lines. There was scant civic spirit. The city grew in a haphazard fashion, with unregulated reclamation of the marshes. There was no aristocratic or wealthy landed presence or no single outstanding merchant family to guide the expansion of the city – the Georgian streetscapes and squares of Dublin and Limerick passed the city by. The Wide Streets Commission, renowned for its corruption, was inactive until well into the nineteenth century. Those few wide streets the city centre possessed were due to the serendipitous arching-over of stinking water channels.[22] Public lighting came to Cork late and its unreliability was a perennial complaint. As well as being often in darkness, the quays were unprotected, and drownings were a depressingly frequent occurrence. It is often claimed that if one were to be transported back in time to the eighteenth century, the feature that would most assail our modern sensibilities would be the all-pervasive stink. In a dirty world, Cork was notorious for the filth that accumulated in private and public spaces, especially the mounds of human and animal waste collected in every laneway, even off the main streets. It is metaphorically appropriate that Cork's best-known public clock was infamous for offering a different choice of time on each of its four faces.

Yet, Cork was a progressive, outward-looking city. Maybe the lack of central authority and regulation released entrepreneurial energies. Every place is, to varying degrees, defined and shaped by its geographical circumstances, but Cork city – located between its rich agricultural hinterland and its commodious harbour – maybe more than most. It liked to proclaim itself the third city of the empire, which in population terms for at least some of the eighteenth century might well have been true. Cork was a nodal point of the Atlantic world, not alone the gateway to the western seas but tightly linked to continental European culture and commerce.

Merchants, trainee priests, men and officers of the British military and the Irish legions, medical students – there was constant movement between Cork and the outside world. John O'Keeffe the actor claimed there was hardly a man of thirty he had met in eighteenth-century Cork that had not lived on the Continent for a period, and many of the women too.[23] During the prolonged French wars, there was a vast concourse of army and navy personnel passing through the city, for stays of short and long durations. The city was abreast of the social and cultural developments of Britain and, in art and literature, punched above its weight. Most of all Cork was characterized by an exploding prosperity, fed by decades of near-continuous war. Haddock's interests and endeavours – the *Androides*, theatre, mineral waters, glass, paper – all were grounded in his Cork experiences and exposures. The ease and success with which Haddock and his activities transferred to Britain and America illustrate how well-integrated Cork was into the wider world.

Haddock was a singular figure. There is no available template into which to squeeze him. He was not part of any movement. If leisure is both a driver and an outcome of Irish identity formation in the nineteenth century, Haddock adds little to the narrative – he is a hanging thread in its complex weave.[24] In Irish terms, he seems an isolated figure. It might reflect his membership of a cohort – a minority group, a non-elite Protestant, from a background of the tradesman/artisan/shopkeeper class, if from the higher grade of that caste – that was never great in size and that subsequently largely petered out. Mechanical exhibition was a niche area that, except for occasional touring productions, made no previous or subsequent splash. He spent most of his career outside Ireland, a stranger in foreign parts. In cold analysis, he might be best viewed as a particular product of the booming war-based economy of his homeplace, that, after Waterloo, lacking an industrial base, went into decline for the rest of the century. He was shaped by a concatenation of influences and factors peculiar to their time and place. His greatest fame was abroad, and he would more neatly fit into an Atlantic-world narrative than an Irish one. The pathway from Ireland to Britain and on to

America is now one well-trodden. Father Mathew a short few years later travelled a similar itinerary, even if the medium and message were different, followed by cultural and other figures, but Marsden Haddock may well have been the first pilgrim on this road to fame and fortune.

Maybe because of these considerations, Haddock has been below history's radar, and has barely figured in the historical record. Fame or popular recognition or historical memory is a poor indicator of achievement, worth or struggle. This work is based on limited materials, largely restricted to newspapers, the occasional handbill and other ephemera. The sources available provide only a framework of a biography. Although we know little of his personal life and motivations, the main message in many ways is his engaging biography. There was something indomitable about Haddock, never constrained by circumstances or mishaps. His adventures in enterprise strayed far beyond the *Androides*. Persevering and never daunted, armed only with ingenuity, energy and determination, he was irrepressible.

The last evidence we have of the *Androides* is that they appeared in an auction in 1834 of the remains of Thomas Weekes, once a rival exhibitor to the *Androides*:

> This exhibition, the invention of the late Mr Haddock, was exhibited with the greatest success some years back, in Norfolk Street, Strand, to very crowded audiences. It consists of a number of small figures, and others the size of life, which go through a series of amusing performances, the whole of which is moved by an invisible agent.[25]

The mystery and, to many, the menace of this 'invisible agent' were the elements of Haddock's entertainment that underlay the public's fascination and the show's popularity – and were also the subject matter of much of the unsolicited verse the *Androides* inspired. Exploring the penumbra between the animate and inanimate, of what distinguishes man from machine, and what makes us human is of increasing relevance to modern culture and society, and to our future. One of the earliest poetic efforts was anonymously published in Bath in 1797:[26]

ART met her sister NATURE late,
And seeing her at ease,
Invited her to take a seat
At her *Androides*;

Dame NATURE went-was pleas'd at first,
And warmly praised her sister;
Then laughing, till she nearly burst,
In seeming rapture kiss'd her.

But as the wond'rous figures work'd
She look'd a little serious,
Whilst envy in her bosom lurk'd
Her brow became imperious.

'How's this!' to ART she loudly said,
'How's this! ungrateful creature!
Profanely thou hast dar'd to tread
Thus in the walks of NATURE'.

'I prithee, base, usurping wench,
No more these freedoms take;
If thus my province thou intrench
Thou'lt men and women make'.

ART seeing NATURE on the rack,
Acknowledg'd thus the whole
'Once, Sister as you turned your back
Your implements I stole.'

And knowing Haddock's skilful hand
Surpass'd my trammel'd rules,
Together we these figures plann'd
But used Dame NATURE's tools.'

'Then be appeas'd', she gently cried,
'Not of this trick complain
Since we, nor mortal hand beside
Shall do the like again'.

Notes

ABBREVIATIONS

BNL   *Belfast News-Letter*
CEP   *Cork Evening Post*
CG   *Cork Gazette*
CMC   *Cork Mercantile Chronicle*
DIB   *Dictionary of Irish biography*
FJ   *Freeman's Journal*
HC   *Hibernian Chronicle (Cork)*
JCHAS   *Journal of the Cork Historical and Archaeological Society*
N&Qs   *Notes and Queries*
NCEP   *New Cork Evening Post*
NUIM   *National University of Ireland, Maynooth*
NYEP   *New York Evening Post*
ODNB   *Oxford dictionary of national biography*
SNL   *Saunders's News-Letter*

INTRODUCTION

1 D. Russell, 'Popular entertainment, 1776–1895' in Joseph Donohue (ed.), *The Cambridge history of British theatre* (Cambridge, 2015), pp 369–87.
2 *HC*, 11 May, 8 June 1789, 25 Jan. 1796; Handbill, *Curiosities of Botany Bay* (Cork, 1789).
3 Alison FitzGerald, 'Astonishing automata: staging spectacle in eighteenth-century Dublin', *Irish Architectural and Decorative Studies, the Journal of the Irish Georgian Society*, 20 (2007), pp 19–33.
4 *HC*, 15 Nov. 1790.
5 *HC*, 3 Sept. 1792.

I. MARSDEN HADDOCK AND CORK

1 *CG*, 6 Sept. 1797; *Cork Journal*, 22 Sept. 1755; *HC*, 1 Apr. 1784, 12 Sept. 1785, 9 Feb. 1786, 5 Apr. 1787, 5 June 1788, 27 May 1790; *CG*, 29 Jan., 30 July 1794.
2 William Sangster, *Umbrellas and their history* (London, 1855), pp 57–64.
3 *HC*, 22 July 1790.
4 *HC*, 6 Oct. 1785, 19 Apr. 1792.
5 Audrey Robinson, 'Anglo-Irish music in Cork, 1750–1800' (MA, NUIM, 1996), pp 6, 30–1, 38–9, 41–2.

6 Robinson, 'Anglo-Irish music', p. 40.
7 F.H. Tuckey, *The county and city of Cork Remembrancer* (Cork, 1980), p. 225; *CMC*, 29 Aug., 3 Dec. 1804.
8 FitzGerald, 'Astonishing automata'.
9 Robinson, 'Anglo-Irish music', p. 40; *HC*, 29 Jan. 1784, 19 Apr. 1792; *CG*, 2 Sept. 1895.
10 Extracts from Cork newspapers *JCHAS*, 41, 1936, p. 46; *CMC*, 28 Sept. 1808; *HC*, 1 Nov. 1790.
11 Robert Day, 'Eighteenth-century trade circulars and invoices of Cork traders', *JCHAS*, 7 (1901), pp 166–71; *HC*, 3, 12 Sept. 1792; *CEP*, 17 Jan. 1793.
12 *CG*, 17 Oct. 1795, 26 Mar. 1796; Ephraim Chambers, *Cyclopædia; or, An universal dictionary of arts and sciences* (London, 1728), p. 87.
13 David Dickson, 'City, season and society' in J.S. Crowley, R.J.N. Devoy, D. Linehan and P. O'Flanagan (eds), *Atlas of Cork city* (Cork, 2005), pp 127–34.
14 *HC*, 21 Apr. 1794; *CG*, 26 Apr. 1794; *HC*, 5 May 1794.
15 *CG*, 15, 22 Aug., 3 Oct. 1795.
16 *CG*, 22 Oct. 1794.

17 *CG*, 24 Sept, 15, 22 Oct., 17, 24 Dec. 1794; *FJ*, 17 Mar. 1795.

18 *FJ*, 17 Mar. 1795.

19 *FJ*, 14 Mar., 9 May 1795.

20 *FJ*, 2, 28 Apr., 18 June 1795.

21 *CG*, 29 Aug. 1795; *HC*, 3 Sept. 1795.

22 *CG*, 15, 22 Aug. 1795.

23 *CG*, 15, 22, 29 Aug., 19 Sept., 3, 10, 16 Oct. 1795; *HC*, 3 Sept. 1795.

24 David Dickson, *Old world colony: Cork and south Munster, 1630–1830* (Cork, 2005), pp 122, 157–8.

25 *HC*, 20 July 1795; see Southwell's entry in *DIB*.

26 Robinson, 'Anglo-Irish music', p. 38.

27 Robinson, 'Anglo-Irish music', pp 38–42.

28 Robinson, 'Anglo-Irish music', pp 40–1.

2. LONDON AND BACK TO CORK

1 *Observer*, 3 Dec. 1797; *FJ*, 14 Mar., 9 May 1795; *Times*, 9 Jan. 1796; H. Houdini, *The unmasking of Robert-Houdin* (New York, 1908), p. 105.

2 *Times*, 28 Apr. 1796.

3 Haddock, advertising handbill, 1800.

4 MIMC, Exhibitions of automata in London, *N&Qs*, 29 Apr. 1925, pp 331–2; R.D. Altick, *Shows of London* (London, 1978), pp 65–6.

5 Lisa Nocks, *The robot: the life story of a technology* (Westport, 2007), pp 30–1.

6 *Observer*, 13 May 1798; *Times*, 8 June 1798; Altick, *Shows*, pp 65–6.

7 Altick, *Shows*, pp 65–6; A. Abrahams, 'Exhibition of automata in London', *N&Qs*, 8 Apr. 1922, pp 269–70; *Observer*, 14, 21 Oct. 1798.

8 *ODNB* entry; MIMC, Exhibitions, *N&Qs*, 1925.

9 Haddock, handbill.

10 *Weekly Messenger*, 9 Nov. 1820.

11 *Hull Packet*, 12 Oct. 1813.

12 *Observer*, 27 Mar. 1796; *Fayetteville Gazette*, 22 Nov. 1820.

13 Haddock, handbill.

14 MIMC, Exhibitions, *N&Qs*, 1925; Houdini, *Unmasking*, pp 116–19.

15 Haddock, handbill.

16 MIMC, Exhibitions, *N&Qs*, 1925; Alison Bames, 'Mathematical water magic', *History Today* (Oct. 2008), pp 8–9; *Charleston Mercury*, 27 Jan. 1823; *Newburyport Herald*, 12 Apr. 1825.

17 Haddock, handbill.

18 *Observer*, 27 Mar. 1796; *Baltimore Gazette*, 9 May 1828; *Sentinel* (Burlington, Vermont), 10 Nov. 1826.

19 MIMC, Exhibitions, *N&Qs*, 1925.

20 *Times*, 18 Dec. 1795.

21 *Times*, 27 Mar., 14 Apr. 1796.

22 *Times*, 27 Mar. 1796; Anthony Pasquin, *A critical guide to the exhibition of the Royal Academy for 1796* (London, 1796); Luke Herrmann, 'Turner at the Royal Academy', *Burlington Magazine* (1975), pp 63–9; *Times*, 23, 28 Apr., 16 May 1796; *Observer*, 5 May 1799, 18 May 1800.

23 *Observer*, 19 June, 3, 17, 31 July, 7, 14 Aug. 1796.

24 *CG*, 30 July 1796.

25 *CG*, 25 Jan. 1797; *Jackson's Oxford Journal*, 15, 29 Apr. 1797.

26 *Observer* 4 June, 6 Aug. 1797; *Times*, 7 June, 22 Sept. 1797.

27 *Observer*, 6 Aug. 1797; *CG*, 25 Jan. 1797.

28 *Observer*, 20, 27 Aug., 17 Sept. 1797.

29 *Observer*, 12 Nov. 1797; see L. Colley, *Britons: forging the nation, 1707–1837* (New Haven, CT, 2014), pp 290–3, 297–306.

30 *Telegraph*, *The handbook of communication* (London, 1842), pp 13–14.

31 *Times*, 27 Dec. 1797.

32 *Observer*, 14 Jan. 1798.

33 *Leeds Intelligencer*, 31 Jan. 1814; *Boston Intelligencer*, 4 Nov. 1820; *New Hampshire Gazette*, 31 May 1825.

34 *Observer*, 15, 29 July 1798.

35 *Times*, 4, 18 May, 5, 8 June, 30 July 1798; *Observer*, 20 May, 3 June, 8 July 1798.

36 *CG*, 11 June 1794, 8, 10 June 1795, 25 Jan., 30 July, 6 Sept. 1797.

37 *NCEP*, Sept. 1798 in Robinson, *Music*.

38 *The Methodist Magazine for the year 1819* (London), vol. XLII, p. 929.

39 *NCEP*, 2 Aug., 24, 27 Sept. 1798.

40 *Observer*, 23 Sept. 1798.

41 Theophilus Marcliffe, *The looking-glass: a true history of the early years of an artist* (London, 1805), pp 80–1.

42 *Observer*, 8 Sept. 1799.

43 *Observer*, 26 Jan. 1800.

44 *Observer*, 2 Feb. 1800; *Times*, 14 Apr. 1800.

45 *Observer*, 25 Nov. 1798.

46 *Kentish Gazette*, 6 Sept. 1799; *Vergennes Gazette*, 7 Nov. 1799.

47 Abrahams, Exhibition, *N&Qs*, 1922; *Observer*, 23 June 1799.

48 *Observer*, 8 Sept. 1799, 9, 30 Mar. 1800; *Times*, 20 May 1800.

49 *Observer*, 8 June 1800, 14 Nov. 1802.

50 Altick, *Shows*, pp 350, 362; MIMC, Exhibitions, *N&Qs*, 1925; *Observer*, 14 Nov. 1802; *Star* (London), 23 Mar. 1805; *Morning Chronicle*, 10 Apr. 1805; Houdini, *The unmasking*, p. 119.

51 Dr Caulfield's annals of the parish church of St Maria de Shandon: *JCHAS*, 10 (1904), p. 275; Holy Trinity minute book, 1820–91, quoted in S. O'Regan, *Music and society in Cork, 1700–1900* (Cork, 2018), p. 57; *CMC*, 29 Aug., 3 Dec. 1804, 14 Sept. 1808.

52 *CMC*, 4, 6 July, 7 Oct. 1803.

53 *Derby Mercury*, 12 Dec. 1816.

54 Andy Bielenberg, *Cork's industrial revolution, 1780–1880: development or decline?* (Cork, 1991), p. 79; C. O'Mahony, 'Bygone industries of Blarney and Dripsey', *JCHAS*, vol. 89 (1984), pp 77–88.

55 *CMC*, 14 Jan. 1803; *British Press*, 11 Oct. 1821.

56 *SNL*, 6, 10 June 1811.

57 R. Knight, *Britain against Napoleon: the organisation of victory, 1793–1815* (London, 2014), pp 410–14.

58 *CMC*, 14 July 1806, 11 May, 13 July 1807, 3 Oct. 1808, 24 Sept. 1813, 3 June 1814.

59 *Holden's Triennial Directory, 1805–1807* (London, 1805), p. 67; W. West, *Directory and picture of Cork and its environs* (Cork, 1810), p. 112.

60 *CMC*, 11 May 1810, 10 Aug. 1812.

61 Bielenberg, *Cork's industrial revolution*, p. 79; O'Mahony, 'Bygone industries'; *CMC*, 4 Mar., 19 Aug., 1811, 13 Sept. 1815.

62 K. Milne, 'First fruits and twentieth parts' in S.J. Connolly (ed.), *The Oxford companion to Irish history* (Oxford, 1998), p. 195.

63 Tuckey, *The county and city of Cork Remembrancer*, p. 242; *CMC*, 5 Oct. 1810, 4 May 1812; *FJ*, 1 July 1811; *BNL*, 14 Feb. 1812; *FJ*, 5 May 1812.

64 Anon., *A description of Mr Haddock's exhibition of Androides; or, Animated mechanisms, also of the telegraph, worked by an automaton, with telegraphic dictionary &c.* (Cork, 1810).

65 *CMC*, 18 Apr., 14, 16, 21 May, 11 June 1810.

66 *Limerick Gazette*, 9 Nov. 1810.

67 *FJ*, 28 Feb., 4 Mar., 25 May 1811, *SNL*, 13 Apr. 1811.

68 *FJ*, 28 Mar., 27 May, 3, 17, 20, 26, 29 June, 1 July 1811; *SNL*, 24 June 1811.

69 *Belfast Telegraph*, 20 Dec. 1811, *BNL*, 3, 10, 17, 24, 28 Jan., 14 Feb. 1812; *CMC*, 4 May 1812.

70 *CMC*, 4 May 1812.

3. TOURING IN BRITAIN AND AMERICA

1 *Caledonian Mercury*, 12 Dec. 1812, 8, 13 Mar. 1813; *Yorkshire Herald*, 21 Aug. 1813; *Hull Packet*, 14 Sept., 26 Oct., 2 and 9 Nov. 1813; *Leeds Mercury*, 18 Dec. 1813, 12 Feb. 1814; *Leeds Intelligencer*, 3 Jan. 1814. http://luddidebicentenary. blogspot.com/2014/02/the-curious-case-of-marsden-haddocks.html.

2 *Liverpool Mercury*, 17 June 1814.

3 *Bristol Times*, 5 Nov. 1814; *Bath Chronicle*, 26 Jan. 1815; *Worcester Journal*, 22 Feb. 1816; John Alfred Langford, *A century of Birmingham life; or, A chronicle of local events, from 1741 to 1841* (2 vols, Birmingham and London, 1868), vol. ii, p. 387; *Leicester Journal*, 27 Sept. 1816; *Derby Mercury*, 28 Nov., 12, 19, 26 Dec. 1816.

4 *Norfolk Chronicle*, 31 May, 28 June, 19 July, 9 Aug. 1817; *Ipswich Journal*, 13 Sept., 18 Oct., 1, 22, 29 Nov. 1817, *Bury and Norwich Post*, 17, 31 Dec. 1817, 14 Jan. 1818.

5 *Kentish Weekly Post*, 15 May, 6 Oct. 1818.

6 Paul Townsend, 'Mathewite temperance in Atlantic perspective' in David T. Gleeson (ed), *The Irish in the Atlantic world* (Columbia, SC, 2010), pp 21–37.

7 David T. Gleeson, 'The Atlantic Irish?' in David T. Gleeson (ed.), *The Irish in the Atlantic world* (Columbia, 2010), pp 3–5.

8 *CMC*, 15 Jan. 1817.

9 *Charleston Daily Courier*, 21 Mar. 1820; National Archives and Records Administration, Film M237, Reel 1.

10 *NYEP*, 26 May, 10 June 1820; *Mercantile Advertiser*, 26 May 1820.

11 *Longworth's American almanack*, New-York register, vol. 48 (1823/4), p. 203.

12 *NYEP*, 23 June 1820.

13 *Boston Daily Advertiser*, 28 Nov. 1820.

14 *NYEP*, 22, 26 May, 17, 23 June, 3 July, 1 Aug. 1820; *Mercantile Advertiser*, 24 June 1820; *Commercial Advertiser*, 5 July 1820.

15   *Boston Intelligencer*, 9, 23 Sept. 1820; *Boston Daily Advertiser*, 21 Apr. 1821.

16   *Poulson's American Daily Advertiser*, 7 June 1821.

17   M237 Roll 2 no. 224.

18   *Poulson's American Daily Advertiser*, 1, 24 Aug., 1, 19, 29 Oct., 12 Nov. 1821.

19   *Baltimore Patriot*, 19 Jan. 1822.

20   *Commercial and Daily Advertiser*, 14 Dec. 1821, 19 Jan. 1822; *Baltimore Patriot*, 15, 22 Mar. 1822.

21   *Baltimore Patriot*, 18, 23 Mar. 1822; *Independent Chronicle and Boston Patriot*, Sept. 11, 1822; *Albany Argus*, 4, 17 Sept., 8 Oct. 1822.

22   *City Gazette*, 18 Dec. 1822; *Charleston Mercury*, 9 Jan., 12, 21 Feb. 1823; *Charleston Daily Courier*, 15 Jan., 24 Mar., 15 Apr. 1823.

23   *NYEP*, 4 Oct. 1823, *American*, 31 Jan. 1824; *Spectator*, 23 Mar. 1824.

24   *Boston Daily Advertiser*, 26 Sept. 1824; *Boston Commercial Gazette*, 23 Dec. 1824, 10 Jan. 1825; *Essex Register*, 14 Feb., 21 Mar. 1825; *Salem Gazette*, 25 Mar. 1825.

25   *Newburyport Herald*, 22 Mar. 1825; *Eastern Argus*, 4 July 1825; *Newburyport Herald*, 23 Sept. 1825.

26   *Boston Patriot*, 9 Nov. 1825; *Rhode Island American*, 20 Dec. 1825; *Rhode Island Republican*, 12 Jan. 1826.

27   William Back, Edward R. Landa and Lisa Meeks, 'Bottled water, spas and early years of water chemistry', *Ground Water*, 33 (1995), pp 605–14.

28   *CMC*, 9 Aug. 1802; 25 Feb., 7 Mar., 11 Apr., 3 May 1803, 20 Aug. 1804.

29   Longworths; *Eastern Argus*, 14 July 1825; *Boston Commercial Gazette*, 12 June 1826.

30   *Boston Commercial Gazette*, 12 June 1826; see www.sodasandbeers.com/Articles/ArticleSoda0001/SABArticles Soda0001_02.htm (accessed 4 Nov. 2017).

31   *Boston Daily American Statesmen*, 9 June 1826; *Boston Commercial Gazette*, 12 June 1826.

32   Her stated age at death does not match that on her disembarkation in America: *Columbian Centinel*, 29 June 1826; *Salem Gazette*, 28 July 1826.

33   *Montreal Herald*, 18 Oct. 1826; *Sentinel and Democrat*, 10 Nov. 1826; *New Brunswick Fredonian*, 24 Jan. 1827; *Poulson's American Daily Advertiser*, 10 Mar. 1827; *National Gazette Philadelphia*, 2 Apr., 17 May 1827.

34   *Poughkeepsie Journal*, 10 Oct. 1827; *Rochester Telegraph*, 24 July 1827; *American and Commercial Advertiser*, 23 Feb. 1828.

35   *Hartford Courant*, 2 Sept. 1828, 5, 19, 26 May 1829.

36   *Observer*, 25 Nov. 1798; *Charleston Daily Courier*, 3 Jan. 1823.

37   *Boston Commercial Gazette*, 2, 6 Mar., 13 Apr. 1826.

38   *Providence Patriot*, 24, 31 May, 3 June 1826.

39   *NYEP*, 25 May, 2 June 1827.

40   *NYEP*, 19 Feb. 1829; G.C.D. Odell, *Annals of the New York stage*, vol. 3: 1821–34 (New York, 1928), pp 407–8.

41   *Derby Mercury*, 12 Dec. 1816; *Boston Intelligencer*, 25 Nov. 1820.

42   *National Gazette Philadelphia*, 14 May 1827; *New Hampshire Sentinel*, 16 May 1828; *Providence Patriot*, 6 June 1827.

43   *Baltimore Gazette and Daily Advertiser*, 21 Apr. 1828.

44   Letter from the secretary of state, transmitting a list of patents ... from the first of January to the thirty-first of December, 1828, inclusive. 8 Jan. 1829. 20th Congress, 2nd Session, B vol. 185, session, vol. 2, H. Doc. 59, 8 Jan. 1829.

45   List of American patents granted in July 1828, *Franklin Journal and American Mechanics' Magazine*, Sept. 1828, pp 211–12.

46   *Boston Masonic Mirror*, 24 July 1830; *Pittsburgh Weekly Gazette*, 17 Aug. 1830.

47   Lyman Horace Weeks, *A history of paper-manufacturing in the United States, 1690–1916* (New York, 1969), p. 189.

48   *Cork Constitution*, 14 July 1829.

49   *Newburyport Herald*, 12 Apr. 1825.

50   *SNL*, 3 May 1811.

51   *Salem Gazette*, 22 Feb. 1825.

52   *Charleston Mercury*, 27 Nov. 1822.

53   *Boston Patriot*, 9 Nov. 1825; *Independent Chronicle*, 9 Nov. 1825.

54   *Poulson's American Daily Advertiser*, 24 Apr. 1822.

55   *Liverpool Mercury*, 17 June 1814; *Boston Patriot*, 15 Sept. 1820.

56   *Belfast Telegraph*, 20 Dec. 1811; *Leeds Intelligencer*, 11 Jan. 1814; *Liverpool Mercury*, 10 June 1814; *Observer*, 9 Dec. 1798.

57   *FJ* 25 May 1811; *Leeds Intelligencer*, 3 Jan. 1813; *Liverpool Mercury*, 26 Aug. 1814.

58 *Hull Packet*, 14 Sept. 1813.

59 *Albany Argus*, 17 Sept. 1822.

60 *Charleston Daily Courier*, 24 Dec. 1822.

61 *Observer*, 13 Jan. 1799; *Leeds Intelligencer*, 3 Jan. 1813; *Commercial and Daily Advertiser*, 22 Feb. 1822.

62 *NYEP*, 11, 22, 29 July 1820; *Poulson's American Daily Advertiser*, 12 July 1821.

63 *Charleston Mercury*, 3 Oct. 1827.

64 *American*, 30 June, 25 July 1820.

65 *Observer*, 23, 28 July 1799; *Columbian Centinel*, 31 Jan. 1821.

66 The quotations of Dr Johnson and a review of eighteenth-century advertising are found in P.M. Briggs, 'News from the little world: a critical glance at eighteenth-century British advertising', *Studies in Eighteenth-Century Culture*, 23 (1994), pp 29–45.

67 Altick, *Shows*, p. 4.

68 James M. Barriskill, 'Newburyport theatre in the early nineteenth century', *Essex Institute Historical Collections*, 93 (1957), pp 311–13; *FJ*, 26 Mar. 1811; *Leeds Intelligencer*, 3 Jan. 1813.

69 *Observer*, 21 Jan. 1798, *Norfolk Chronicle*, 30 Aug. 1817.

70 *The Ricky Jay Collection*, Sotheby's auction, 27 Oct. 2021; Sotheby's auction catalogue, Hodgson's Rooms 1979, p. 48, lot 1241.

71 Alison FitzGerald and Joy Sherwood, 'The business of leisure: entertainment ephemera in the collection of the Royal Irish Academy' [blog], 27 Aug. 2019: www.ria.ie/news/library-library-blog/business-leisure-entertainment-ephemera-collection-royal-irish-academy.

72 Anon., *A description*.

73 *BNL*, 18 Feb. 1811, *Boston Intelligencer*, 28 Apr. 1821; *Repertory*, 8 May 1821; *An account of the Boston Asylum for Indigent Boys* (Boston, 1831), p. 22; *American*, 20 Apr. 1824; *Salem Gazette*, 29 Mar. 1825.

74 Briggs, 'News from the little world'.

75 *FJ*, 25 May 1811.

76 Russell, *Popular entertainment*, p. 386; Hugh Cunningham, *Leisure in the Industrial Revolution, c.1780–c.1880* (London, 1980), p. 35.

77 Anon., *A description*.

78 *Columbian Centinel*, 19 May 1821; *Boston Commercial Gazette*, 1 Nov. 1821.

79 *Boston Intelligencer*, 28 Apr. 1821; *Boston Daily Advertiser*, 8 May 1821, *Repertory*, 8 May 1821; Anon., *An account*, p. 22.

80 *Charleston Daily Courier*, 18 Dec. 1822; *Charleston Mercury*, 22 Jan. 1823.

81 *City Gazette*, 18 Dec. 1822; *Centinel of Freedom*, 12 Dec. 1826; *Poughkeepsie Journal*, 10 Oct. 1827; *Connecticut Journal*, 1 July 1828; *Connecticut Courant*, 19, 26 Aug. 1828, 12 May 1829.

82 *Yorkshire Herald*, 21 Aug. 1813; *Bury and Norwich Post*, 7 Jan. 1818.

83 *Observer*, 4 Nov. 1798; *Montreal Herald*, 18 Oct. 1826; *Rochester Telegraph*, 26 July 1827.

84 *Commercial Advertiser*, 13 July 1820; *Columbian Centinel*, 20 Sept. 1820; *Baltimore Patriot*, 15 Jan. 1822; *Essex Register*, 14 Feb., 17 Mar. 1825; *Newburyport Herald*, 12 Apr. 1825.

85 *Poughkeepsie Journal*, 17 Oct. 1827; *Baltimore Patriot*, 23 Feb. 1828; *Albany Argus*, 27 Sept. 1822; *Charleston Mercury*, 21 Dec. 1822; *FJ* 14 Mar. 1795; *Columbian Centinel*, 20 Sept. 1820.

86 *Jackson's Oxford Journal*, 15 Apr. 1797; *Times*, 7 June 1797; *Caledonian Mercury*, 14 Dec. 1812; *Leeds Intelligencer*, 3 Jan. 1813; *Hull Packet*, 21 Sept. 1813; *Leeds Mercury*, 24 Dec. 1813; *NYEP*, 26 May, 17 June 1820; *Baltimore Patriot*, 14 Dec. 1821; *City Gazette*, 18 Dec. 1822; *Observer*, 6 Aug. 1797.

87 *Ipswich Journal*, 25 Oct. 1817; *Charleston Mercury*, 22 Jan. 1823.

88 *Baltimore Patriot*, 11 Mar. 1822.

89 Barriskill, 'Newburyport theatre', pp 311–13.

90 *Baltimore Gazette*, 15 Apr. 1828.

91 Odell, *Annals of the New York stage*, p. 114.

92 *Times*, 26 Mar. 1799.

93 *FJ*, 16 Apr. 1811.

94 *Observer*, 15 July 1798; *Baltimore Patriot*, 15 Feb. 1822.

95 *FJ*, 5 June 1811; *Observer*, 13 Jan., 7 July 1799, 19 Jan. 1800.

96 *Columbian Centinel*, 31 Jan. 1821.

97 *FJ*, 28 Apr. 1795; *Leeds Intelligencer*, 27 Dec. 1813; *Observer*, 31 July 1796; *Charleston Daily Courier*, 18 Dec. 1822.

98 *FJ*, 28 Apr. 1795; *NYEP*, 10 June 1820.

99 P. Clark and R.A. Houston, 'Culture and leisure, 1700–1840' in Peter Clark (ed.), *The Cambridge urban history of Britain*, vol. 2: *1540–1840* (Cambridge, 2008), p. 576.

100 *CMC*, 16 June 1802.
101 L.M. Cullen, 'Patrons, teachers
      and literacy in Irish: 1700–1850'
      in Mary Daly and David Dickson
      (eds), *The origins of popular literacy in
      Ireland: language change and educational
      development, 1700–1920* (Dublin, 1990),
      p. 39; E. Wakefield, *An account of Ireland
      statistical and political*, 2 (London, 1812),
      pp 766–7; *HC*, 2 Feb. 1772.

CONCLUSIONS
1   *NYEP*, 10 June 1820; *American*, 12 June
      1820.
2   M. Kang, *Sublime dreams of living machines:
      the automaton in the European imagination*
      (Cambridge, MA, 2011), pp 185–222.
3   *Observer*, 25 Nov. 1798.
4   *CG*, 26 Aug. 1795.
5   *Liverpool Mercury*, 19 Aug. 1814.
6   G. Wood, *Edison's Eve* (New York, 2002),
      p. xv.
7   *FJ*, 20 June 1811; *NYEP*, 10 June 1820.
8   *Observer*, 1 July 1798.
9   *Observer*, 11 Mar. 1798.
10   *Salem Gazette*, 4 Mar. 1825.
11   *Baltimore Gazette*, 7 Apr. 1828.
12   *Newburyport Herald*, 12 Apr. 1825.
13   *Boston Intelligencer*, 4 Nov. 1820.

14   *NYEP*, 10 June 1820.
15   *Eastern Argus*, 11 July 1825.
16   *Salem Gazette*, 15 Mar. 1825.
17   MIMC, Exhibitions, *N&Qs*, 1925.
18   *Observer*, 6 Aug. 1797.
19   *Connecticut Mirror*, 18 Aug. 1828.
20   *NYEP*, 10 June 1820.
21   Altick, *Shows*, p. 76.
22   David Dickson, 'Large-scale developers
      and the growth of eighteenth-century
      Irish cities' in P. Butel and L.M. Cullen
      (eds), *Cities and merchants: French and Irish
      perspectives on urban development, 1500–1900*
      (Dublin, 1986), pp 109–10, 117.
23   *Recollections of the life of John O'Keeffe*,
      vol. 1 (London, 1826), p. 236.
24   L. Lane and W. Murphy, 'Introduction'
      in L. Lane and W. Murphy (eds), *Leisure
      and the Irish in the nineteenth century*
      (Liverpool, 2016), pp 1–19 at pp 3–6.
25   Ricky Jay, *Extraordinary exhibitions: the
      wonderful remains of an enormous head,
      the whimsiphusicon & death to the savage
      unitarians: broadsides from the collection of
      Ricky Jay* (New York, 2005), p. 54; *New
      Times*, 2 July 1824.
26   *Bath Herald*, 28 Jan. 1797. This version
      taken from Anon., *A description*,
      pp 19–20.